Tragic Ways of Killing a Woman

Tragic Ways of Killing a Woman

NICOLE LORAUX

Translated by Anthony Forster

HARVARD UNIVERSITY PRESS
Cambridge, Massachusetts
and London, England

Originally published as *Façons tragiques de tuer une femme;* © 1985 Hachette.

First Harvard University Press paperback edition, 1991

Set in Galliard and designed by Joyce C. Weston.

Library of Congress Cataloging-in-Publication Data

Loraux, Nicole.
Tragic ways of killing a woman.

    Translation of: Façons tragiques de tuer une femme.
    Bibliography: p.
    Includes index.
    1. Greek drama (Tragedy)—History and criticism.
2. Women in literature. 3. Death in literature.
4. Sacrifice, Human, in literature. 5. Suicide in
literature. I. Title. *1991*
  PA3136.L6713 1987 882'.01'09 87-390
  ISBN 0-674-90225-4 (alk. paper) (cloth)
  ISBN 0-674-90226-2 (paper)

CONTENTS

PREFACE

"DEATHS represented on the stage, great suffering, wounds": events of tragedy, a *spectacle*. As one considers the examples given by Aristotle to support his definition of tragic *pathos* as "action causing destruction or suffering,"[1] how can one possibly doubt that in the Athenian theater death was meant to be seen? *Thanatoi en tōi phanerōi:* death agonies in public, a murder in front of everybody . . . As I reread Aristotle's sentence, I am puzzled, and I realize that I should warn the reader that in these pages it is the listener to tragedy who will take precedence over the spectator, because everything comes to us through words. Everything happens in words, and this is particularly true of death. In trying to define the ways in which women die in Greek tragedy, I have found nothing that is seen by the audience, or at least nothing that is seen in the first instance: everything starts by being spoken, by being heard, by being imagined. For seeing is born from words and is closely bound up with them. This is why, in the course of my reading, I felt that I could make out under the surface of the words what it was that gave the Greek audience some particular moment of intense pleasure in listening.

So words are read to replace, if not to recover, words that were heard, words to which the Athenian public listened closely in the tragic performance. Those words could be heard in more than one way, in many different ways: in short, a text and nothing but a text. My choice may be to rely "much more on imagination than on sight, more on the ear than on the eye,"[2] but what difference does it make? It happens that this was also the choice made, in fifth-century Athens, by tragedy itself. I am not going to bring forward proof of this; it would need much more than a preface. Just as a reminder, and for general interest, I will mention some of the reasons for making tragedy mainly a matter of listening.

There are, first of all, some historical reasons. A profound, Cratylean sense of having roots in their language was natural to the Greeks, and they loved their words (which they called "names"). We must remember how extensively in fifth-century Athens the rules of listening dominated those civic orations that we rather inaccurately call a literary genre. I would go so far as to say that in the Athenian theater listening was, for the tragic audience, like a sensitive reading, on a par with the "depth" of the text.[3] In fact, if we follow Jean-Pierre Vernant and think of the member of the ancient audience as a listener with sharp hearing for whom "the language of the text would be transparent at every level, with all its polyvalence and ambiguities,"[4] we have to credit this all-powerful listener with an attention that, to say the least, could not have been very free-floating; credit him, too, with resources of memory such as we no longer command. He must have had an astonishing ability to compress the long business of unraveling the complexities of the signifier into the short span of a theatrical performance. A fiction, perhaps, but a necessary fiction, which the reader must use when he begins to lose himself in the polysemic depth of the text and the endless quest for resonant echoes.

The historian has now slipped away from the scene. The text remains, and people who are going to do something with it at the present time. In the forefront of them are the director and actors. We should not really hope that they are going to give substance to the idea of its being a spectacle.[5] If we question him, the director will admit the difficulty that he has in persuading his actors to speak—simply to speak, and not to act—the great textual units that make up a tragedy, such as the chorus in the *Agamemnon* on the sacrifice of Iphigenia, the account of Deianira's death in the *Trachiniae,* or the sacrifice of Polyxena in the *Hecuba.*[6]

So it remains for the reader to put his entire trust in the text. Indeed, as a reader of the tragedies I had no choice in the matter. I was forced to do so from the moment that I had to admit, in trying to bring out the ways in which women die in Greek tragedy, that these ways were to be found in the text. I found nothing but recitals of events. It was as if female death could be entrusted only to words; that only words could see it through. There were historical reasons for this, of course, reasons arising from social conditions. It was in the depths of her house that a Greek woman was supposed to live out her existence as young girl, as wife, and as mother; and it was shut up in her house, far from the gaze of others, that she had to end her life. All this is true; but propriety, even when founded on sociology, has never been able to explain everything.

One can easily accept that the sacrifice of a virgin—that sheer deviation—can happen only in narrative. So tragedy puts virgins on the stage only to remove them and deliver them out of sight to the slaughterer's knife. An outrageous execution becomes a satisfying fiction, the stages of which are described by messengers in a technical language that loads an unthinkable act with all the weight of reality. It is a fruitful act to kill young girls in imagination, in a narrative. But there was also the suicide of wives, and this complicates matters for us, in that it, too, was described and not shown to the audience. Was it because they were on the brink of a social transgression that these desperate women had to fly to their quarters—shadowy, hidden, mysterious—to put themselves to death, so that a nurse or an attendant had to come and tell the public what they had done? Undoubtedly, it is this reluctance to die in public that marks the limit of the invention of femininity in tragedy: the way in which distraught wives go back to conventional life in order to end it. But this is not all. To have recourse to the order of language[7] in order to kill Phaedra or Deianira may be one of the constitutive features of tragedy in its Greek form. At least one should not underestimate the real benefit, in terms of the imagination, that these deaths, and the fact that they were only described, must have brought to an audience of citizens.

In connection with these deaths that are put into words I would repeat what Baudelaire said about beauty, when he defined it as "lending itself to conjecture." Death by report lends itself to conjecture vastly more than does violence exposed to the public view. In itself the setting of women on the stage was already an excellent opportunity for the Athenian citizen to ponder the difference between the sexes. It was a chance to state the difference before obscuring it, and then to find it again, all the richer for having been obscured, and more firmly based for having been finally reaffirmed. The death of a woman, however, because it dramatizes and concentrates all the elements of this development, is the ideal place for this process of the imagination. This is all the more true in that tragedy uses for the spoken description words of multiple meaning, words that are somehow "in the know."[8]

There are precise words, such as *aiōra* and *airesthai*, which have a technical meaning in religious and sacrificial language;[9] very general words, such as *bainein*, a colorless description of the act of walking ("she is gone, the wife . . ."); names of "regions of the body"—the throat, for example.[10] All these words are used in tragedy and are deflected to provide the texture of a discourse which can be clearly heard and which, under the surface of speech, always proclaims the difference between the sexes. So it is by examining the texts word for word that I have tried to understand what, within the performance, is at work in the words when a messenger describes the death of a woman.

It is now time to come to the text.

However, I would not like to embark on this long-term study without thanking those to whom I communicated all or part of my researches for their suggestions and remarks—in my seminar at the Ecole des Hautes Etudes en Sciences Sociales and at the universities of Toulouse, Trieste, Cornell, Princeton, and Harvard. And I am particularly grateful to those who invited me to come and speak about the death of women in tragedy, and so gave me the chance to write these pages: Gregory Nagy in the first instance, and Claudine Leduc. My thanks go also to Maurice Olender, to whom this book owes its existence, and to Patricia Williams, who welcomed it warmly to Harvard University Press; to Anthony Forster, who devoted all his skills as a translator to these pages; and to Claire Forster and Bernard Williams, for their vigilant and enlightened advice.

Tragic Ways of Killing a Woman

INTRODUCTION

I N GIVING their lives for their city, the Athenians who fell in war won "unfading praise and the most glorious of burial-places—I do not mean the place where they rest, but the renown they have left behind, which will be remembered forever . . . For the whole earth is a burial-place for famous men, and, to proclaim what they were, it is not enough to have an inscription engraved on a stone in their own country. In foreign lands an unwritten memorial of the choice they made dwells in all and everyone." These are words of Pericles, as Thucydides reports his funeral oration (IV.23.2–3): words on the death of a group of men.

Compare what a fragment of an epitaph has to say about the death of one woman in the same city, Athens: "Time will never, Nicoptoleme, efface the eternal memory of your worth, the memory that you bequeathed to your husband."[1] The men died in a war fulfilling the civic ideal to the utmost. The woman, submitting to her destiny, died in her bed—at least that is what is most likely. To the men the city gave a fine burial-place and a panegyric in the form of an *epitaphios* delivered by the leading politician of the day; and what is more, the eloquent words of Pericles declared that the epitaph engraved on the Kerameikos monument would pale by comparison with the universal and imperishable renown of these heroes. As for Nicoptoleme, unknown despite her warrior name that tells of victory in battle, a brief

I

private memorial was enough—a few lines engraved on a funeral stone, and the statement that her husband will never forget her. A stark contrast, too striking perhaps to be absolutely typical. And yet . . . Certainly not all Athenian men died in battle, but every epitaph shows in one way or another that the city would always remember the qualities of the dead man. Not all Athenian women died in their beds, but it was always left to the husband, or at least to the family, to preserve the memory of the dead woman.

At the level of social expectations, the city, in effect, had no comment to make on a woman's death, even if she was as perfect as she could be. A woman was allowed no accomplishment beyond leading an exemplary existence, quietly as wife and mother alongside a man who lived the life of a citizen. Quietly—this at any rate was the life that Pericles recommended, in his funeral speech, to the widows of Athenians fallen in battle. The glory (*kleos*) of men lived on, carried to the ears of posterity by the thousand voices of renown. The glory of a woman had no spokesman but her husband, ever since Penelope stated that only the return of Ulysses would revive her diminished *kleos* (*Odyssey* XIX.124– 128). It was the husband who, after the death of his wife, would be the repository of her memory. If she survived her husband, it was for a woman not to get herself talked about among men, in terms of either praise or blame. The glory of a woman was to have no glory.[2] This certainly does not make any easier the task of someone who wants to probe the silent reality of women's lives in Athens. But this is not my intention, and I shall stick resolutely to the *logos,* even if it means basing myself on a literary genre that in Athens granted to the death of women a treatment completely different from the private one of intimate mourning.

However, although it complicates the problem, we must consider briefly how to read epitaphs. They give the impression that a woman could not control her own death. For someone whose virtues had to concentrate on the well-being of her husband, there was no heroic end: if a "fine death" is seen as a qualifying test, it was a man's preserve. The death of a wife simply drew to a close a life of love and devotion, of good humor and discretion; and a husband would know, afterward, how "to speak very well" of that life.

In these conditions, what sort of public statement could be made about the death of a woman? Certainly not historical writing, especially if the historian were called Thucydides and the subject were Greece. Because it is a recital of wars and political decisions, the Thucydidean treatment of history made no mention of women, even in their lifetime. As one might expect, Herodotus was less categorical, but predictably he was interested only in women who were barbarians or the wives of tyrants, or who died violent deaths; or he made a woman's death an excuse for mentioning an unusual funeral rite.[3] Even so, the accounts are only brief and do not display any great elaboration. But there was a genre that, as a civic institution, delighted in blurring the formal frontier between masculine and feminine and freed women's deaths from the banalities to which they were restricted by private mourning. This was tragedy, where, as indeed in Herodotus, women died only violent deaths:[4] but in the world of tragedy, even if death was encountered on the field of battle, it was always classed as violent, and men suffered from this convention no less than women. So, for a while at least, a balance was reestablished between the sexes.

Women in tragedy died violently. More precisely, it was in this violence that a woman mastered her death, a death that was not simply the end of an exemplary life as a spouse. It was a death that belonged to her totally, whether, like

Sophocles' Jocasta, she inflicted it "herself upon herself"[5] or, more paradoxically, had it inflicted upon her. It was a brutal death, whose announcement was curt—thus for the wife-and-mother of Oedipus "one word is enough, as brief to utter as it is to hear: she is dead, that noble figure Jocasta"; but the manner of the death, painful or shocking, gave rise to a long recital. For the event, as soon as it was announced in its stark nakedness, evoked a question that was always the same: "How? Tell us, how?"[6] So the messenger gave an account, and it was thus that tragedy broke the silence that was widely observed in the Greek tradition on the manner of death.

In tragedy women's deaths are described in the same way as men's. But there is still a distinction to be made: in the type of violent death, there is in practice a difference between men and women, and here the balance between the sexes is broken again. On the men's side, death, with few exceptions—such as the deaths of Ajax and Haemon, who committed suicide, and that of Menoeceus, who offered himself up as a sacrificial victim—takes the form of murder. Thus it was a case of murder, but family murder (*oikeios phonos*), when the sons of Oedipus, technically as warriors, killed each other on the field of battle. As for women, some of them were murdered, such as Clytemnestra and Megara, but many more had recourse to suicide, as the only escape in a desperate misfortune—Jocasta and, again in Sophocles, Deianira, Antigone, and Eurydice; Phaedra and, again in Euripides, Evadne and, in the background of the *Helen,* Leda. Finally, in the case of young girls, the sacrificial knife was the favored instrument of death, and, to the host of wives who killed themselves, one must add the group of virgins who were sacrificial victims, from Iphigenia to Polyxena and including Macaria and the daughters of Erechtheus.

I shall not be particularly concerned with murder, though I shall sometimes mention the forms it takes in tragedy. As murder was more evenly divided between men and women, it is certainly less relevant to distinguishing between the sexes in their relations to death. Where the deaths of women are concerned, the suicide of wives and the sacrifice of virgins must obviously engage most of our attention.

· I ·

The Rope and the Sword

A Woman's Suicide for a Man's Death

"For a woman it is already a distressing evil to remain at home, abandoned, without a husband. And when suddenly one messenger arrives, and then another, always bringing worse news, and all proclaiming disaster for the house . . . ! If this man had received as many wounds [*traumatōn*] as were reported to his home through various channels, his body would now have more cuts [*tetrōtai*] than a net has meshes . . . Those were the cruel rumors which made me more than once hang my neck in a noose, from which I was wrenched only by force" (Aeschylus, *Agamemnon*, 861–876).

Beyond the lie that the queen handles with consummate skill, there is a truth, or at least an apparent truth, proper to tragedy, which is expressed in these words of Clytemnestra as she welcomes Agamemnon on his return to his palace. The death of a man inevitably calls for the suicide of a woman, his wife. Why should a woman's death counterbalance a man's? Because of the heroic code of honor that tragedy loves to recall, the death of a man could only be that of a warrior on the field of battle. Thus the children of Agamemnon in the *Choephoroe* dream for a moment of what might have been their father's glorious death under the walls of Troy; and, on merely being told of her husband's death, his wife, immured in her home, would kill herself with a noose round her neck. It was as part of this tragic pattern that Hecuba in the *Troades* (1012–14) was bitterly to rebuke Helen because nobody had ever "surprised her in the act of hanging up a noose or sharpening a dagger as a noble-hearted woman [*gennaia gynē*] would have done in mourning her first husband."

Of course Clytemnestra did not kill herself, any more than her sister Helen did. Not only was the queen no Penelope (even though in her lying speech she speaks of her eyes burning with tears as she lay sleepless, crying for her absent husband), but she was also no ordinary tragic wife. Clytemnestra did not kill herself, and it was Agamemnon who was to die, ensnared in her veil and his body pierced with wounds. She turned death away from herself and brought it upon the king, just as Medea, instead of killing herself, was to kill Jason indirectly through his children and his newly-wed wife.[1] In Clytemnestra, the mother of Iphigenia and the mistress of Aegisthus triumphed over the king's wife. The murdering queen denied the law of femininity, that in the extreme of misery a knotted rope should provide the way out.[2]

A Death Devoid of Male Courage

Finding a way out in suicide was a tragic solution, one that was morally disapproved in the normal run of everyday life. But, most important, it was a woman's solution and not, as has sometimes been claimed, a heroic act.[3] That the hero Ajax, both in Sophocles and in the epic tradition, killed himself was one thing; that he killed himself in a virile manner was another, and I shall come back to this. But to infer from this example that in the Greek imagination all suicide was inspired by *andreia* (the Greek word for courage as a male characteristic) is a step we should not take. Heracles in Euripides without doubt conforms much more to the traditional ethic when, from the depths of his disasters, he agrees to go on living.[4] In the case of mere citizens, things are even clearer. Nothing was further from suicide than the hoplites' imperative of a "fine death," which must be accepted and not sought.[5] We know that after the battle of Plataea the Spartan Aristodamus was deprived by his fellow citizens of the posthumous glory of appearing on the roll of valor because he had sought death too openly in action. Whether he were a Spartan or not, a warrior committed suicide only when struck by dishonor, as Othryadas did in book I of Herodotus and Pantites in book VII. Plato in the *Laws* echoes these practices; he is prescribing laws but is loyal to civic conventions when he lays down that the suicide should be formally punished, "for total lack of manliness," by being buried in a solitary and unmarked grave on the edge of the city, in the darkness of anonymity (IX.873c–d). I would add (and it is relevant) that the Greek language, in the absence of a special word for suicide, describes the act by resorting to the same words as are used for the murder of parents, that ultimate ignominy.[6]

Suicide, then, could be the tragic death chosen under the weight of necessity by those on whom fell "the intolerable pain of a misfortune from which there is no way out."[7] But in tragedy itself it was mainly a woman's death. There was one form of suicide—an already despised form of death—that was more disgraceful and associated more than any other with irremediable dishonor. This was hanging, a hideous death, or more exactly a "formless" death (*aschēmōn*), the extreme of defilement that one inflicted on oneself only in the utmost shame.[8] It also turns out—but is it just chance?—that hanging is a woman's way of death: Jocasta, Phaedra, Leda, Antigone ended in this way, while outside tragedy there were deaths of innumerable young girls who hanged themselves, to give rise to a special cult or to illustrate the mysteries of female physiology.[9]

Hanging was a woman's death. As practiced by women, it could lead to endless variations, because women and young girls contrived to substitute for the customary rope those adornments with which they decked themselves and which were also the emblems of their sex, as Antigone strangled herself with her knotted veil. Veils, belts, headbands—all these instruments of seduction were death traps for those who wore them, as the suppliant Danaids explained to King Pelasgus.[10] To borrow Aeschylus' powerful expression, there was here a fine trick, *mēchanē kalē,* by which erotic *peithō* (persuasion) became the agent of the most sinister threat.

I am not going to dwell here on women's relation to *mētis,* that very Greek concept of cunning intelligence. Yet this is a good moment to recall that, even when a woman was armed with a sword to kill herself or another, every action of hers was likely to be covered by the vocabulary of cunning. Thus, in the *Agamemnon,* in order to suggest the murderous designs of Clytemnestra as she sharpened her sword for use against her husband, Cassandra quite unexpectedly resorts to the imagery of poison mixed in a cup. But the text of the *Oresteia* will soon substitute a very real snare, the garment that will imprison Agamemnon as in a net—a bold materialization of every metaphor concerning *mētis.* The same logic is at work in the *Trachiniae.* Without meaning to, Deianira has caught Heracles in the poisoned trap of Nessus' shirt. She straightway turns to the sword for a quick death and her release, but even so her suicide can still be construed, if only momentarily, as the product of cunning intelligence.[11]

Against this ensnaring *mētis,* which works in the words and actions of women and weaves the meshes of death or busily tightens knots, tragedy sets up in contrast the weapons that cut and tear, those that draw blood. This brings us back to the Suppliants of Aeschylus and their drive toward hanging. As a last resort in their headlong flight from the sons of Aegyptus, the deadly rope would protect the Danaids against the violent desire of the male, just as hurling themselves from the top of a steep rock (something they dreamed for a moment of doing) would have kept them safe from marriage, that prison where the husband is only a master. But it is significant that they give this master the name of *daiktor*, which does not mean "ravisher" (as an influential translation has it) but, very precisely, "tearer."[12] From this tearing—which clearly refers to rape or deflowering—there are only two ways of escape: either the death of the Danaids by the rope, resulting in defilement of the city, or their survival at the cost of a war that would spill the blood of men "on behalf of women" (*Supplices* 476–477). The Danaids did not hang themselves. We know the result—marriage arranged in the end, a wedding night ending in bloodshed, fatal for the husbands, and later punishment in Hades. But that is another story.

The Gash in the Man's Body

If we are to believe Euripides, Thanatos (Death) was armed with a sword. This was certainly not pure chance. If death, the same for all, makes no distinction between its victims and cuts the hair of men and women alike, it was for Thanatos, the male incarnation of death, to carry the sword, the emblem of a man's demise.[13]

A man worthy of the name could die only by the sword or the spear of another, on the field of battle. The Menelaus of Euripides was an inglorious character, being the only warrior to come back from Troy without even a trace of a wound suffered in close combat, the only wound that made a man complete.[14] Even in human sacrifice, an act that was corrupt from every point of view, the executioner had to be a man, especially when the victim was a male. There is proof of this in *Iphigenia in Tauris,* where Orestes questions the sister whom he has not yet recognized: "Would you, a woman, strike men with a sword?" and Iphigenia assures him in reply that there is a male killer (*sphageus*) in the sanctuary to carry out the task.[15]

Even suicide in tragedy obeys this firm rule, that a man must die at a man's hand, by the sword and with blood spilt. In Sophocles, as in Pindar, Ajax kills himself by the sword, faithful till the end to his status as a hero who lives and dies in war, where wounds are given and received in an exchange that, on the whole, is subject to rules. So Ajax kills himself, but in the manner of a warrior.[16] Pierced by the blade with which he identifies himself (*Ajax* 650–651), he tears open his side on the sword that, in staging his own death, he makes into an actor: "the killer [*sphageus*] is there," he says, "standing upright so that he can slice as cleanly as possible."[17] Ajax's sword is a basic signifier in Sophocles' play, recurring at each step in the metaphorical texture of the tragedy and serving to bind it together. If it is the warrior's sword itself that becomes the healing blade that Ajax invokes in his prayers, there are also in a figurative sense many other swords in the *Ajax,* such as the words that have been sharpened like steel and "cut the living flesh." No wonder then that, at the sight of the hero's corpse, the sharp blade of grief pierced Tecmessa "to the liver."[18]

I shall say no more about Ajax's sword. Others before me have discussed it ably, sometimes brilliantly like Jean Starobinski.[19] Nor shall I dwell on the theme of spilt blood, even though it is central to the *Ajax,* for there is another of Sophocles' heroes to make the point that a man's suicide is inevitably bloody. This is the betrothed of Antigone, whose death is announced punningly in words that cannot adequately be translated: "Haemon is dead; his own hand has drenched him in blood."[20] It is enough to recall that the name Haemon is only too like the word for blood (*haima*). In this way the son of Creon, pierced by his own sword, fulfills the prophecy of his own name and dies like a man.

Hanging or Sphagē

There is a word that must now be mentioned, because it is obsessively present in Greek tragedy and is insistently opposed to the language of hanging. This word is *sphagē*, which means sacrificial throat-cutting, and also the gash and the blood that flows from it. Together with the verb *sphazō* and its derivatives, it is of course used to indicate sacrifices—the sacrifice of Iphigenia in Aeschylus and Euripides, but also in Euripides that of Macaria in the *Heraclidae,* of Polyxena in the *Hecuba* and the *Troades,* of Menoeceus in the *Phoenissae,* and finally of the daughters of Erechtheus offered to their country by way of *sphagia* (*Ion* 278). Up to this point there is nothing abnormal to note, or scarcely so. But, from Aeschylus through Sophocles to Euripides, *sphazō* and *sphagē* are also used to denote murder within the family of the Atreides. Moreover, the same words are used to describe a suicide when it is stained with blood, such as the suicides of Ajax, Deianira, and Eurydice. In order to justify this slight deviation from the usual meaning, can one call on some principle of semantic looseness in the character of tragic speech? Is *sphazō* to be lumped together with words that are more neutral or descriptive like *schizō* and *daizō*, which imply tearing of the body?[21] This would be a misunderstanding of the verbal rigor of Greek tragedy, which twists language only for a very definite purpose, such as to upset the normal categories. It is better to trust in the strong sacrificial sense of these words and to notice that *sphazō, sphagē,* and *sphagion,* terms laden with religious values, do not signify in tragedy just any throat-cutting murder or suicide, but the long series of "murders that result from the application of the blood law" in the family of the Atreides, or the self-inflicted death of Eurydice at the foot of the altar of Zeus Herkeios.[22] More generally, *sphagē* is used to characterize death by the sword as a "pure" death in opposition to hanging.[23]

No sooner have we recalled this difference between two modes of death, one male and the other female, than we are forced to admit that the distinction is in fact violated in the "virile" deaths of Deianira and Eurydice, who plunge swords into their bodies. And in Euripides there is no lack of heroines who, as they contemplate death, prefer the sword to the rope. Thus Electra, as she mounts guard at the door of the house where Clytemnestra is being murdered, brandishes a sword, ready to turn it on herself if the enterprise should fail (*Electra* 688, 695–696). (Conversely, in Euripides there are men who die fatally strangled, in the manner of women. Thus Hippolytus, entangled in the reins of his horses, was smashed against the rocks by the roadside.[24] However, as far as men were concerned, it must be said that this irregular form of death was evidently less frequent.)

The confusion in tragedy that consists in giving a man's death to a woman is not a matter of chance. Let us take the death of Jocasta in the *Phoenissae.* In Sophocles, as we all know, as soon as Jocasta came to see the truth about Oedipus, she hanged herself, as a woman overwhelmed by a crushing misfortune. The Jocasta of Euripides did not hang herself. She survived the revelation of her incest and it was the death of her sons that killed her, as she turned on herself the sword that had killed them.[25] This was a remarkable departure from a tradition that had been well established since Homer and the hanging of Epicaste (Jocasta). Should one attribute this innovation, as some do, to a change in outlook that had become increasingly hostile to death by hanging?[26] There is really nothing to support this hypothesis: ever since the *Odyssey* (XXII.462–464), the rope dealt the impurest of deaths, and one cannot see how attitudes could have developed on this point. But above all one should read the text of Euripides beside that of Sophocles, and one will see that the *Phoenissae* brings a whole new interpretation of the character of Jocasta. She is no longer, as she is in Sophocles, above all a wife; she is exclusively a mother,[27] and her manly death should be seen as a consequence of this critical reshaping of the tradition.

Starting from this example and several others, I offered in an earlier publication a generalization about women's deaths in tragedy, to the effect that hanging was associated with marriage—or rather, with an excessive valuation of the status of bride (*nymphē*)—while a suicide that shed blood was associated with maternity, through which a wife, in her "heroic" pains of childbirth, found complete fulfillment.[28] I still abide by that reading. However, I shall not return to it, for it is simply the confusion as such that interests me here, and more particularly the many statements in Euripides that seem to assume that the rope and the sword come to the same thing.

The rope or the sword—in brief, death at any price, whatever the method. That is the way manlike women, who would in general prefer the sword, reason in a desperate situation. It is also the way women who are overfeminine boast when, like Hermione, they will not dare even to hang themselves. But, in either case, the way the text runs makes it perfectly clear what would be the real choice for the particular woman in despair—the sword or the rope. It is this choice that the chorus leaves to Admetus, in face of the imminent death of Alcestis, saying that "a misfortune of this kind justifies cutting one's throat [*sphagē*] or slipping a noose round one's neck"—a simple way of indicating that, having avoided death, a womanish man would not be able to escape the distress that breaks women's spirits.[29]

Paradoxically, as these few examples have already suggested, the confusion even at its very height aims only to reinforce the standard opposition. So it is with Helen in the play that bears her name, summoning death in her prayers: "I shall put my neck in a deadly, dangling noose, or in a mighty effort I shall sink the whole blade of a sword in my flesh, and its murderous thrust will open up a stream of blood from my throat, and I will sacrifice myself to the three goddesses" (353–357). As the final outcome indicates, the only possibility that Helen sees as truly worthy of her is *sphagē*; but, on closer inspection, the choice was already revealed through the very words in which Helen spoke of hanging herself, and especially in the expression *phonion aiōrēma* (353), the untranslatable and contradictory "gory suspension" that translators cover up as best they can, because in their view the distinctive feature of hanging is that no blood flows.[30] But it is precisely in this oxymoron that one can and must guess what the heroine's choice will be. For her no death can be considered that does not shed blood, and her words reject hanging at the very moment that she mentions its possibility. *Phonion aiōrēma:* proclaiming in advance the blood of the *sphagē,* Helen's language runs ahead of her thought.

At the end of this inquiry, therefore, the contrast between the rope and the sword stands more strongly than ever. But certain facts must be clearly understood. A man never hangs himself, even when he has thought of doing so;[31] a man who kills himself does it in a manly way. For a woman, however, there is an alternative. She can seek a womanly way of ending her life, by the noose, or she can steal a man's death by seizing a sword. Is this a matter of identification, of personal coherence in her character within the play? Perhaps. The imbalance is nonetheless obvious, proving, if proof were needed, that the genre of tragedy can easily create and control a confusion of categories, and also knows the limits it cannot cross. To put it another way, the woman in tragedy is more entitled to play the man in her death than the man is to assume any aspect of woman's conduct, even in his manner of death. For women there is liberty in tragedy—liberty in death.

The Wife in Flight

As there is an alternative open to women, and as some of them choose the ways of femininity to the very end, the question of hanging and of the values associated with it deserves a little more attention.

Beyond the vocabulary of *mētis* and the judgment that it inevitably involves a death where the victim is trapped in her own snare, there is another word that deserves our attention because it describes and suggests rather than judges. The word *aiōra* (or *eōra*) evokes a double image, of a corpse hanging in the air, and of its movement, a gentle swaying.[32] *Aiōra* was in fact the name of a festival at Athens in which representations of hanging were associated with a game on a swing. This religious Aiora is not itself in question here, but rather the visual image induced by the use of the word in tragedy. *Aiōra* of Jocasta and *aiorēma* of Helen: Oedipus has forced open the door that Jocasta had carefully closed on herself, and now everyone can see the woman hanging, "caught in the noose that swings" (*plektais eōrais empeplegmenēn*). For Helen, equally, who did not hang herself, hanging was summed up in the term *aiōrēma*. It is at this point that the reader of tragedies recalls the word from another context, of the woman who throws herself to her death. In the *Suppliant Women* of Euripides, as Evadne prepares to hurl herself into the fire from the top of an airy rock (*aitheria petra*) that dominates the funeral pyre of her husband, Capaneus, she cries: "Here I am on this rock, like a bird, above the pyre of Capaneus, I rise lightly, upward on a deadly swing [*aiōrēma*]" (1045–47).

Aiōrēma signifies both the swaying of the hanged woman and the soaring flight of Evadne, and we should pause at this: in the language of tragedy there is a thematic relationship between hanging and throwing oneself to one's death. This may seem surprising. The woman who has hanged herself has certainly thrown herself into the void, but her body has left the ground—it is supported, now, by the roof. To throw oneself down, on the other hand, is to fall into the depths (*bathy ptōma*). The same word, *aeirō*, which means elevation and suspension, applies to these two flights in opposite directions, upward and downward, as though height had its own depth: as though the place below—whether it be the ground, or the world under that—could be reached only by first rising up.[33] Strange as it may seem, this is the logic that alone makes sense of the association between these two ways of rising, an association that recurs in the "escape odes," those lyrical pieces in which often the chorus and sometimes that tragic heroine, overwhelmed by events, voice their desire for a merciful flight into death. The *Supplices* of Aeschylus may be mentioned here, and the *Hippolytus* of Euripides, and there are many other texts as well. The vital point is that for both movements the same image returns—that of winged flight and, explicitly, the flight of a bird. If Evadne is a bird, so is Phaedra—recently a bird of ill omen, and now a pathetic bird escaped from the hands of Theseus. Falling from the heights of a rock or held in the noose, it makes no difference: Evadne and Phaedra have taken flight, forever. There are women, too, who go no further than dreaming of flight, such as Hermione, who in her desire for death wishes she were a bird; or the Danaids, distraught at the approach of men; or again the women of the chorus in *Iphigenia in Tauris* or *Helen,* wingless halcyons burning with regret for their far-off country.[34]

The bird is in tragedy an operator that stands for escape, and because it presents a concrete image of flight, it provides several suggestions on what is said about women in connection with hanging.[35] These wives (who were properly represented in everyday life as sedentary) show in their propensity for flight a kind of natural rapport with the beyond: there they are, throwing themselves into the air and hanging between earth and sky. Again, a misfortune was enough to make them escape from a man, abandoning his life, and their own, as abruptly as they left the stage. Identified as he was with the hoplite model, a man had to hold his ground and face death head on, as Ajax at his end rejoins the earth, fastened to it by his sword, which is at once fixed in the ground and plunged to its hilt in his body.

For women, death is an exit. *Bebēke,* "she is gone," is said of a woman who dies or has killed herself. It is said of Alcestis, and of Evadne, who with a leap (*bebēke pēdēsasa*) left her father's house to reach the rock from which she was to throw herself, with another leap, the last (*pēdēsasa*). Theseus, too, as he mourns the death of Phaedra, who "like a bird escaped from one's hands has disappeared," cries out: "A sudden leap [*pēdēma*] has carried you off to Hades."[36] But one must remember about these heroines that, although for a woman death is always a movement, the only ones to take flight are those who are too feminine. In fact the announcement of the death of Deianira, who preferred the sword to the rope, starts as one might expect, but ends on an unusual note: "She has gone, Deianira, on her last journey, her very last, on motionless foot [*Bebēke . . . ex akinētou podos*]" (*Trachiniae* 874–875).

The motionless foot of Deianira may be (as Jebb has suggested) something like a proverbial euphemism for death, a way of indicating that the journey and the road are purely metaphorical . . . I myself would prefer to see the phrase, in its opposition to the flight implied in *aiōra*, as a way of suggesting, even before the chorus speculates on how she died, that Heracles' wife has not fled by hanging herself, and that she has died like a soldier. But, conversely, we must come back to the martial suicide of Ajax: Sophocles, in his treatment of this death, still manages to remind us that for a man suicide is a deviation. The hero's death was indeed a manly one, with this difference, that it was the sword that stood (*hestēken*) in the hoplite's place: Ajax transfixed himself on it, hurling himself with a swift leap, and it is no surprise that this leap is called a *pēdēma*.[37]

This is a good place to notice again that, if in tragedy male and female behavior can disregard the division of humanity into men and women, this shift is not an accident, since it serves to show how each character—whether by conformity or by deviation—lives out a destiny as an individual man or woman. There are dimensions of both reality and imagination to these lives, while the city would like to make them fundamentally a matter of social reality.

In any case, whether they are womanly or manlike, women have at their disposal a way of dying in which they remain entirely feminine. It is the way they have of acting out their suicide, offstage. It is meticulously prepared, it is hidden from the spectators' view, and it is in its main details recounted orally. The staging in Sophocles even follows a standard sequence—a silent exit, a choral chant, and then the announcement by a messenger that, out of sight, the woman has killed herself.

Silence and Secrecy

Silence is the adornment of women. Sophocles said so, and Aristotle repeated it. In Euripides, Macaria, as she prepares to take an active role, makes a point of showing her awareness of this sentiment, remarking that the best thing for a woman is not to leave the closed interior of her house.[38] But women in tragedy have become involved in men's world of action and have suffered for it. So, silently, the heroines of Sophocles return to die in the home that they had left behind. Silence of Deianira under the accusations of Hyllos; heavy silence of Eurydice, in which the chorus correctly divines a hidden threat; half-silence of Jocasta, with ambiguous words and a voice that finally dies away.[39]

These silences, which are heard as expressions of anguish, precede an action that the woman wants to hide from view. Phaedra has made herself invisible (*aphantos*) and Deianira has disappeared (*dieistōsen*): she has organized, one might say, her final disappearance, which takes her far from mortal view to the invisible world of Hades, away from all eyes, even those in the palace where she has taken refuge.[40] In the same way Jocasta and Phaedra hide behind closed doors, which are hermetically sealed on death—an obstacle that puts the body, in hanging, into a double prison. Oedipus has to throw himself against the door, Theseus has to storm and beg that the bolts be drawn back,[41] so that at last they can see their wives—dead. The spectators did not see Jocasta's body, but they do see Phaedra's, and that of Eurydice, revealed to them and Creon at the same time. It was for the messenger to emphasize the effect: "You can see her; for she is no longer in her retreat [*en mychois*]."[42]

An astonishing interplay of the seen and the hidden, by which we do not see a woman's death, but do see the dead woman. Then, as though the last ban had been lifted on staring at this mournful scene, the dramatic action could continue—even, as it does in the *Hippolytus,* center itself on the corpse of the dead woman and her silent presence. Phaedra had disappeared, but her corpse was there, released from the fatal noose to be laid out on the ground as was seemly—the corpse which she had wanted to make into evidence against Hippolytus and which, though silent forever, yet bore the message of the absent woman.[43] That was, without the shadow of a doubt, a very feminine way of exploiting one's own death. In the case of Ajax, whose dead body was at least as important a dramatic element as that of Phaedra, things are very different, and what is seen and what is hidden do not bear at all the same relation to one another. As Ajax is the model of the manly suicide, it follows that he has the right to kill himself in front of the spectators;[44] but because his death is only a poor imitation of a warrior's noble death, there is a ban on seeing his body. Indeed, before the leaders of the Greek army start to discuss whether the dead body would be appropriately hidden in a tomb, Tecmessa and then Teucer have each taken good care to cover up a sight that was as painful as it was improper.[45]

Finally, there is the very special oscillation between revelation and concealment that occurs in the case of Alcestis, who dies in place of a man. Alcestis dies onstage, and her body, first carried inside the palace and then brought back, is displayed onstage again for a long *prothesis* (exposure) before the funeral cortège (*ekphora*) takes it out of sight—for good, the chorus supposes; and it is true that, without the intervention of Heracles, Alcestis would certainly have disappeared forever.[46] But she was an exception, the only woman not to reach Hades. We will confine ourselves to the host of women in tragedy who go away and never return.

In the Thalamos: *Death and Marriage*

Let us come back to the door of that closed place where a woman takes refuge to die, far out of sight. With its solid bolts that have to be forced back for the dead woman to be reached—or rather the dead body from which the woman has already fled—this room reveals the narrow space that tragedy grants to women for the exercise of their freedom. They are free enough to kill themselves, but they are not free enough to escape from the space to which they belong, and the remote sanctum where they meet their death is equally the symbol of their life—a life that finds its meaning outside the self and is fulfilled only in the institutions of marriage and maternity, which tie women to the world and lives of men. It is by men that women meet their death, and it is for men, usually, that they kill themselves.[47] By a man, for a man: not all texts make the distinction, but Sophocles is particularly careful to mark it—in the *Antigone,* where Eurydice dies *for* her sons but *because* of Creon, and in the *Trachiniae,* where Deianira dies *because* of Hyllos but *for* love of Heracles. So the death of women confirms or reestablishes their connection with marriage and maternity.

The place where women kill themselves, to give it its name, is the marriage chamber, the *thalamos.* Deianira plunges into it, as does Jocasta. Alcestis sheds her last tears there before facing Thanatos; and when she leaves the palace to die, it is toward this place that she turns her thoughts and her regrets. As for the funeral pyre of Capaneus, onto which Evadne hurls herself to renew her union in the flesh with her husband, it is decribed as *thalamai* (funeral chamber), a word that encapsulates the many connections of her death with marriage.[48]

If the *thalamos* is in the depths of the house, there is also within the *thalamos* the bed (*lechos*), scene of the pleasure that the institution of marriage tolerates if it is not excessive and, above all, the place of procreation. No death of a woman takes place without involving the bed. It is there, and there alone, that Deianira and Jocasta are able, before suicide, to affirm their identity to themselves.[49] It is there that Deianira even dies, on that couch that she had too much associated with the pleasures of the *nymphē*. Even when a woman kills herself like a man, she nevertheless dies in her bed, like a woman.

Finally, by fastening the rope to the ceiling of the marriage chamber, Jocasta and Phaedra call attention to the symbolic framework of the house. The rooftree, which the *Odyssey* called *melathron,* Euripides calls *teramna*. By metonymy it can mean the palace considered in its dimension of verticality; but it goes even further. From Sappho's epithalamium ("Come, carpenters, lift up the rooftree [*melathron*], Hymenaeus, for here enters the house a bridegroom the equal of Ares") to Euripides, the roof seems to have been much connected with the husband, whose tall stature it dominates and protects.[50] One might perhaps recall that Clytemnestra, in her irreproachable speech that is also a total lie, called Agamemnon "the column sustaining the high roof" (*Agamemnon* 897–898). Just before a woman leaps into the void, it is the missing presence of the man that she feels for the last time, in every corner of the *thalamos*.

To Die with . . .

It is no wonder, then, if many of these solitary deaths were thought of as ways of dying with one's husband. To die with: a form in death of *synoikein,* "to live with," which was one of the commonest expressions in Greek to mean marriage.[51]

To die with . . . It was certainly not the fate that Clytemnestra sought, for she much preferred to live with Aegisthus than to die. However, it was the lot that Orestes, with cutting irony, singled out for Clytemnestra when, just before striking her, he told her to go and sleep in death with the man she loved and preferred to her own husband. A just turn of events in the logic of the *Oresteia,* a just retribution for the death of Cassandra at Agamemnon's side, a death that a short while back Clytemnestra had presented as the fate deserved by a mistress.[52] To die with . . . The fate that, in the *Oresteia,* is imposed on women by the logic of murder becomes, in the case of female suicides, the object of a will that seems at once like love and like despair. The moment Deianira knows that disaster is on its way, she announces to her confidantes, the women of Trachis, her intention of joining Heracles in death: "I have decided that, if misfortune befalls him, I too shall die with him, in the same impulse, the same moment" (*Trachiniae* 719–720). This is a firm intention, expressed four times within the same line, and she will carry it out in every respect, except that the word "with" will have meaning only for herself. Because she robs Heracles of a man's death, the hero when he is laid low will deny her, condemning her beyond death to the solitude that was her lot in life. Euripides' Helen, too, should be mentioned, who does not die but talks much of dying. Like the virtuous Helen of Stesichorus in her Egyptian exile[53] she swears that, if Menelaus dies, she will kill herself with the same sword and rest at her husband's side. Finally, as any conduct has its extremes, Evadne deserves a special mention, who, in a bacchantic ecstasy of conjugal love, turned the funeral pyre of Capaneus into a shared tomb.

Not content with aspiring to die with the man who was dear to her, she dreamed of annihilation in an erotic union of their two bodies: "In the burning flame I shall mingle my corpse with my husband's, resting close against him, flesh to flesh."[54]

To die with . . . A tragic way for a woman to go to the extreme limit of marriage, by, it must be said, drastically reordering events, since it is in death that "living with" her husband will be achieved. Yet there is one woman, a mother rather than a wife—or, more precisely, a mother to excess—who displaces "dying with" in the direction of maternity. I mean the Jocasta of Euripides, who, in keeping with her destiny as an incestuous mother, dies with the death of her sons and, "dead, rests on her well-loved ones, embracing them both in her arms."[55] This is how in the *Phoenissae* Euripides reconstructs the story of Jocasta, who, by marrying her son, mingled marriage with motherhood and so could die only as a mother. Moreover the men to whom women offer up their deaths can represent either of two relationships, as we have seen; and when it comes to dying, a Eurydice may prefer death for her sons' sake to life with her husband. Jocasta is original because she "dies with" those whom she brought into the world, killing herself on their bodies, at the very place where they died in battle.

The Glory of Women

The time has come to bring out what tragedy's treatment of the death of women borrows from socially accepted norms in classical Athens, and what separates it from them. What is at stake is the thorny question of the "glory of women" (*kleos gynaikōn*); even the most routine formulation of this is not entirely covered by Pericles' terse declaration.

The funerary epitaphs, which represent a traditional ethic, are not so uncompromising, where women's glory is concerned, as the radicalism of Pericles in his funeral speech. The idea is not completely strange to them, but this glory, which is always subordinated to a career as a "good wife," often merges into feminine "worth" (*aretē*). This means that the glory of women is often mentioned in a tentative, not to say reticent, manner. Female worth is never confused with real worth, which belongs to men and in their case needs no further specification. There is no male worth, there is simply *aretē* itself.

Listen to the words of mourning in their orthodox form:

> Supposing that feminine virtue still exists in the human race, she partook of it

cautiously says an epitaph from Amorgos; and an inscription from the Piraeus goes further:

> Glykera was found to have a double gift, which is rare in women's nature—virtue allied to chastity.

In the praise and admiration of mankind that are sometimes accorded to a wife, her death, that final accident, counts for nothing and the life she led for everything. This is the sentiment in another epitaph from the Piraeus:

> What is in the world the highest praise for a woman Chairippe received in the fullest measure, when she died.

Still more explicit is the epitaph engraved on the tomb of an Athenian woman:

> It was you, Anthippe, who in the world had the most acclaim open to women. Now that you are dead, you have it still.

So much for the daily glory of women. This may have been, for Athens, substantial, but it is also very little. It is true that "good" wives are not material for tragedy.

This does not mean that women in tragedy are not wives. But they are wives in their deaths—and apparently only in their deaths, because only their deaths belong to them, and in them they bring their marriages to fulfillment. It follows that we can take two views of their deaths, contradictory but at the same time complementary. The first, which is attuned to traditional values, holds that in fulfilling themselves as spouses in their deaths the heroines of tragedy are confirming tradition at the very moment that they are innovating. The second view, which is anxious to lay hold of anything in tragedy that tends to support the "women's side,"[56] takes the point that wives in death win a renown that goes far beyond the praise traditionally granted to their sex. It is not necessary to choose one view over the other: each has its truth, and in fact it is impossible not to accept, in each case, both at once. This is what is meant by ambiguity, and there must have been an ambiguous thrill to the *katharsis* when, during a tragic performance, male citizens watched with emotion the suffering of these heroic women, represented onstage by other male citizens dressed in women's clothes. Women's glory in tragedy was an ambiguous glory.

Take the case of Alcestis, an exemplary figure in this interpretation of marriage through death. The chorus readily says of her that "of all women she behaved the best toward her husband." Her last word is to say to her husband "farewell" (*chaire*), just like those fair effigies on the stelae in Athenian cemeteries. And yet this irreproachable figure of Alcestis strikingly shows the way in which the glory of women is always twisted. Alcestis was devoted, loving, and virtuous, but she earned her "glorious death" only through the male qualities of courage and endurance. Since a fine death is essentially virile and the loyal wife has taken the man's place, this *tolma* has the recoil effect of feminizing the well-loved husband. He is driven to become the mother as well as the father of their children, and condemned to live henceforward cloistered like a virgin or chaste as a bride inside the palace, which his wife has left to join in death the open spaces of manly heroism.[57]

The glory of Evadne is also very ambiguous. She wants to die as both wife and warrior. To honor her marriage the wife of Capaneus seeks death like some equivocal hoplite who has strayed from the scene of battle. She stands on the steep rock, longing for a tomb to share with her husband and anxious that all Argos should know of her fate, yet decked like a woman who wants to seduce—like a *nymphē* perhaps. As a result, the victory that she claims as her due takes her far beyond the limits of her sex, which usually makes its mark at the loom or by a prudent reserve. When Evadne maintains that her victory is one of *aretē,* neither the woman nor the warrior in her seems to get much from it. For the chorus, made up of mothers in mourning, does not really believe either in her virtue as a woman, which is tainted by excess, or in her courage, whose "virility" is unseemly in the good wife she professes to be.[58]

There is also the belated glory of Deianira, who waits until she has committed the irreparable act before proclaiming her wish for a good reputation (*Trachiniae* 721–722). Above all, there is the strange paradox of Phaedra's glory. As infatuated with glory as she was with Hippolytus, Phaedra dies for having lost her reputation as the wife of Theseus. But her death, which she stages in the noble manner, is still an act of *mētis:* the noose she ties round her neck is to prove a trap for Hippolytus, the written note she leaves is to proclaim a false story. Yet her name will achieve renown, because of this love, which she thought would ruin her honor, and because of this disastrous death. This is the height of contradiction. Of course Aphrodite had a hand in all this, but Phaedra herself was to a great extent responsible.[59]

In the matter of femininity, tragedy is two-faced . . . Although they are "out of place," the glories of these women give food for thought; they are to be listened to and seen. Yet, whether excessive or inadequate as wives, Phaedra, Deianira, Alcestis, and Evadne still die within the orbit of marriage. We should accept that tragedy constantly disturbs the norm in the interest of the deviant, but at the same time we must be aware that under the deviant the norm is often silently present. So we have tried out two possible readings at once. One of them draws up a list of all the distortions that, in a system of values, can be applied to those values; the other lends an ear to the occasional dissenting voice in the unison of Greek *logoi* about women.

· II ·

The Pure Blood of Virgins

WITH the *jeunes filles en fleurs,* it is sacrifice and spilt blood that predominate. Because, even in the world of tragedy, they have less autonomy than wives, virgins do not kill themselves: they are killed.

Although I make this generalization, I do not forget that there is at least one virgin who is a striking exception— Antigone, of course, who was not content simply to kill herself, but killed herself in the manner of grieving wives, who hang themselves as a last resort. The difficulty is a real one, and it would be pointless to try to play it down. The least we can do is to undertake a detailed analysis of the conditions attending Antigone's death, which was a mixture of a very female suicide and something like a sacrifice outside the norm. Although he thought he had taken care not to engage his own personal responsibility and that of the state, Creon actually condemned Antigone to Hades, a young life offered as a victim to the gods below.[1] Buried alive, the daughter of Oedipus was doomed to die by suffocation, and in making a noose of her virgin's veil she brought on suffocation by other means. She gained twice, by contriving her own death, and by condemning Creon to the defilement that he wanted to avoid. But the significance of this hanging is not exhausted in the gesture by which Antigone, faithful to the logic of Sophoclean heroines, chose to die by her own will and so to change execution into suicide. By killing herself in the manner of very feminine women, the girl found in her death a femininity that in her lifetime she had denied with all her being; she also found something like a marriage. I shall come back to that last point, but it is important, in the case of this exceptional death, to emphasize from the start that it was an exception, and to point up this strange rule in tragedy that virgins must die by execution.

For that is indeed the rule—or what passes for a rule in the world of tragedy: a sacrifice is made, usually with blood shed, and the victim is a young girl.

Sacrifices Fruitful for Thought

Consider the death of Iphigenia under the sacrificial knife, an exemplary death that none of the three great tragedians failed to recount, and more than once. The death of Iphigenia was a sacrifice, but the victim was a young girl and not an animal. Was this just a trivial detail? One might think so since, to describe Iphigenia's death, tragedy resorts naturally to the verbs *sphazō* and *thyō,* which as a rule signify throat-cutting and the sacrificial act. But there are passages in the plays that see this detail as an enormity and class Iphigenia's death as murder (*phonos*).[2]

The sacrifice of a virgin in the theater allows one to think the unthinkable, to question the normal from the standpoint of extreme abnormality, all the more freely since this abnormality is so flagrant. In an effort to conceal the murder lurking beneath the sacrifice, the religious procedure in Greek cities was to ensure that the animal's slaughter should be strictly stage-managed.[3] The practice of tragedy was to flout these pious precautions and, obedient to the myth, to deliver young girls to the slaughterer's knife. Then the unthinkable became a recital of events, for in these deaths of virgins nothing was seen by the spectators and everything was entrusted to the power of words. It was a recital that was good to hear because theater is fiction.[4] Of course, in real life the city did not sacrifice its young girls, but during a performance it gave its inhabitants the double satisfaction of transgressing in imagination the taboo of *phonos* and of dreaming about virgins' blood.

There is much that could be said about this cathartic interplay of the imaginary, the forbidden, and the real; much too about the function of the theater, that stage set up by the city for the tangling and untangling of actions that anywhere else it would be dangerous or intolerable even to think about. It is not, however, tragedy's view of sacrifice that interests us now, but the set of procedures that, from Aeschylus to Euripides, attend the death of young girls. Since it is also a question of the significance of the figure of the *parthenos,* we shall ask what it is, from mythology to tragedy, that makes a virgin the appointed victim of a sacrifice that breaks the rules.

Iphigenia, Macaria, Polyxena, the daughters of Erechtheus, all these were virgins offered up to bloodthirsty Artemis, to the fearsome Persephone, or to the denizens of Hades, for the safety of the community; so that a war should start or, on the contrary, end; so that a decisive battle should take place and victory come to the side of those performing the sacrifice. Why, on all these occasions of *sphagia,* is it the *parthenoi* that merit the grisly honor of being delivered up to the killer's knife? First of all we should remember that, because she is ignorant of marriage and the works of Aphrodite, the young girl is assumed by the collective imagination to have connections with the world of war. Athena, virgin and warrior, comes to mind. But Athena is a goddess, while Iphigenia, Macaria, Polyxena, and the daughters of Erechtheus are mere mortals. It is the privilege of the goddess to fight battles, while it is the fate of the mortals to be sacrificed. The virgins cannot fight alongside the men, but, in times of peril, their blood flows so that the community of *andres* may live.[5] Sometimes a band of "chosen" (*logades*) is near at hand to see that the sacrifice is correctly carried out, an élite of young warriors whose vocation for death is even more binding than that of other warriors. If defeat should occur, the "chosen" will fight to the last. But to ensure victory, the "chosen" will lead a chosen virgin to the sacrificial knife.[6]

If, therefore, men's blood is not to be spilt in vain, the blood of a virgin must flow. It must be virgin blood, or, as the sacrificers proclaim as they go about their work, "pure blood."[7] Nevertheless such logic, always situated in mythical times, belongs to the imaginary. Whatever liberties tragedy takes with actual social practices, no spectator would forget that, even when in peril, the city usually contented itself with sacrificing animals and that, considered by the ordinary standard of sacrificial systems, the immolation of a virgin was, to put it mildly, an anomaly. Is it to resolve this discrepancy between the real and the imaginary that tragedy, from Aeschylus to Euripides, inclines, through metaphor, to animalize the doomed virgins?

Heifer and Filly, Captured and Tamed

In the *Agamemnon* of Aeschylus, Iphigenia struggled "like a goat," and her father committed her to death "like a beast [*boton*] taken from a flock."[8] Euripides for his part twice compares her to a heifer (*moschos*), indeed a "heifer of the mountains come down virgin from a rocky cave."[9]

The goat was always sacrificed at the critical moment when the battle was starting, and it was no ordinary victim. With the heifer, the method of sacrifice would be more correct if the victim were not defined as a mountain animal. Since the rules required that only a domestic animal could be sacrificed, it was clear that a mountain heifer was not in order. The mountains made wild things out of every creature that lived in them, and, unless one was a Hermes who knew how to juggle the rules like an artist,[10] the sacrifice of a mountain cow was not feasible. Comparing Iphigenia to an *oreia moschos* was a way of underlining the abnormality of all human sacrifice, "the savagery of the victim taking over from the savagery of the act."[11] Furthermore, the outcome of the tragedy confirms this analysis. When finally Artemis, or the poet, substitutes for the young girl a mountain hind to die under Calchas' knife, untamed nature has irreversibly made its way into the heart of the sacrifice.

When Polyxena is due for sacrifice by the Achaeans, she, like Iphigenia, is compared to a mountain heifer; and through this analogy her immolation is placed at the crossroads of the civilized and the savage. However, a simile may not be an adequate figure of speech for Polyxena. Perhaps because no displacement of her fate to another creature should be allowed to sweeten it, she is more readily thought of in terms of metaphor—she *is* the heifer of Hecuba, but she *is* also her "filly" (*pōlos*).[12] Let us consider this word a moment, if only to recall other very similar situations where it is also used to describe a young victim. A case in point is Creon's son, Menoeceus, a candidate for sacrifice and also identified with a colt (*Phoenissae* 947). But the same metaphor can be reversed in a context, such as historical writing, in which real events are more of a limiting factor. Then it is no longer the young girl who is a filly, but the filly who is a young girl. This is how Pelopidas took it when, bidden to sacrifice a "fair-haired virgin," he cleverly interpreted the oracle by immolating a chestnut filly (Plutarch, *Pelopidas* 20–22).

The horse is no more an ordinary sacrificial victim than are animals that are wild or have turned wild. It has its place in military sacrifices, a place certainly more ambiguous than the goat's. However, we shall concentrate on *pōlos* and on the special connotations of this word, which do not necessarily cover the whole field of images associated with the horse. As we ask ourselves what makes Polyxena or Menoeceus a *pōlos,* the emphasis shifts from a contrast between the wild and the tame to an opposition between what has, and what has not, already been tamed.[13] Polyxena is the untamed filly, Menoeceus the unbroken colt. These metaphors show not only that these people are suitable victims for an unorthodox sacrifice, but also that they are candidates for marriage. In brief, for them as for Iphigenia at Aulis, marriage and sacrifice closely interact. Waiting for the domestication of marriage, the young girl is readily compared to an unbroken mare or to a heifer that has not felt the yoke.[14] But the sacrificial victim must also, by definition, be untouched by the yoke, so it is natural—at least if we follow the metaphorical line of the text—that the *pōloi* and *moschoi* destined to have their throats cut will substitute sacrifice for marriage.[15]

However, we must not be mistaken: if for Iphigenia as well as for Polyxena marriage and sacrifice are inextricably joined, one should see in this more than a poet playing variations on a very important metaphor. Indeed, if the theme of sacrifice turns on animal metaphor, it is because, like the victim, the girl is a passive, docile creature, to be given and led away. More precisely, sacrifices in tragedy illuminate the customary ritual in marriage whereby the virgin passes from one *kyrios* (guardian) to another, from the father, who "gives her away," to the bridegroom, who "leads her off."[16] Hence the tragic irony of those funeral processions that ought to have been wedding processions—

those of Iphigenia and Polyxena, and also of Antigone.[17] They are weddings in reverse in that they lead toward a sacrificer, who is often the father,[18] and (as we shall see) toward the home of a bridegroom called Hades. There is a tragic irony, too, in the gesture of Achilles' son "taking the hand" of Polyxena to place her on the top of his father's funeral mound.[19] When the victim is a virgin, the sacrifice is tragically ironic in that it resembles, all too closely, a marriage.

Putting to Death as Marriage

If we are to cast light on this resemblance, we should not hastily attribute it to some general system by which Eros is invariably connected with Thanatos.[20] If we generalize too hastily and are satisfied with the "obviousness" of a few great universal laws, we run the risk of simply forgetting the language—the Greek language, but above all the language of tragedy—in which the equivalence of putting to death and marriage is expressed. So, instead of leaping to conclusions, we should once again move slowly through the word-play of the tragic signifier.

One image stands out clearly at once—the virgins who are led to their deaths are brides for Hades. In the shared understandings of social life, death is a natural metaphor of marriage because, in the course of the wedding procession, the young girl renounces her self. Thus at Locris the bride was taken to be imitating Persephone, who was carried off by her bridegroom who came from the world below.[21] But it is a great advantage of fiction that it can reverse the normal order of discourse, as tragedy does when, in sending young girls to their death, it turns the metaphor round: virgins in tragedy leave for the abode of the dead just as they might their father's home for the home of their husband,[22] and this can happen whether their unspecified destiny is to find "marriage in Hades" (Euripides, *Troades* 445) or to find it in union with Hades himself.

Marriage *in* Hades, union *with* Hades. At the heart of the sacrifice, or of being put to death, the tragic destiny of the *parthenoi* is played out against this background tension between "in" and "with." It is as though every virgin had to find her final fulfillment in marriage, and besides the two alternatives of a "weak" or a "strong" version of death as marriage,[23] there was, it seems, no third possibility. So Antigone, who died for putting a dead brother before life as a spouse, was confronted in death with a marriage, whether she was expected to "find a husband in Hades," as Creon put it, or was promised directly to the lord of the dead. Before dying she had given her husband in the underworld the name of Acheron, but in the messenger's speech it was Hades himself whom the young girl (*korē*) found "in her nuptial chamber carved from the rock."[24] So, dead in the arms of her betrothed Haemon, she is lost to him, but he will still kill himself to join her, driven by a frantic desire to wed her "in the house of Hades" (Sophocles, *Antigone,* 1240–41). Iphigenia, again, came to Aulis to marry the best of the Achaeans, and her husband would turn out to be "Hades and not Achilles."[25]

With Iphigenia, however, we meet more recondite figures of speech, fitting the deadly equation of nuptials and throat-cutting. We should particularly attend to Agamemnon's lament as he weeps in vain over the fate of his daughter, for what it expresses is perhaps more than a simple reference to Iphigenia's marriage in the underworld. At one point the king cries out: "As for the unhappy virgin—virgin [*parthenos*], did I say? It seems that Hades will marry her before long" (*Iphigenia in Aulis* 460–462). Are we to take this cry as nothing but a variation on the theme of marriage with Hades? Or should we find meaning in Agamemnon's reticence and understand that in a sacrifice a virgin loses her virginity? By themselves, these two lines from *Iphigenia in Aulis* would not be enough to endorse that suggestion, but there are two other passages in Euripides in which a sacrificed virgin, without actually being declared the wife of Hades, is still considered to have lost her virginity. This happens to Polyxena, although she does not, in Euripides, become united with Achilles at her death.[26] It was Polyxena, formerly a *nymphē* fit for a king, who in her pride consented to offer up to Hades only her body (*demas*) and on no account her person. At the moment of death, she says only that she is going away "beneath the earth, without husband, without marriage." Yet after her immolation Polyxena will be described by her weeping mother as "a bride without husband, a virgin who is no longer a virgin" (*nymphē anymphos, parthenos aparthenos*).[27]

Of course, in the case of Polyxena, the commentator who is impatient with such an enigmatic phrase can get out of it by reading into Euripides' text the Hellenistic romance of Polyxena's marriage in death with Achilles. He will say that in death "the women-captives became their master's concubines"[28] and will think that he has solved the difficulty by promising the young Trojan woman to the Greek hero's shade. But the problem arises again in a more acute form with the virgin Macaria in the *Heraclidae*. Macaria was not offered in marriage to a hero, but sacrificed to Kore; she refused to be united with the husband of the death goddess, and for her, Hades was only the name of a place; she renounced marriage to save her people and the lives of her brothers. Macaria was the perfect *parthenos*. And yet, when she speaks of the glory arising from her choice and the funeral honors that will be hers, the virgin Macaria goes on to say that for her "this treasure will take the place of children and virginity" (*anti paidōn . . . kai partheneias*).[29] It is awkward for translators and commentators alike. If a virgin is prepared to take glory in place of children she will never have, this may seem to be in the nature of things, since, in the translators' and commentators' view, a woman—and especially a Greek woman—could not expect to have everything. But how is fame supposed to "take the place" of virginity for that wise virgin Macaria? A naive question, and some dispose of it by giving *anti* (in place of) two very different meanings: when it applies to "the children," it introduces a precious possession replaced by glory, but in its application to "virginity," the idea of an incomplete condition that a *parthenos* would want to exchange as soon as possible for fulfillment in marriage. On this reading—at once psychologizing and *petit bourgeois*—funeral honors become a "compensation" for this forced virginity.[30] As none of this is very convincing, nor does it accord with the grave seriousness of Heracles' daughter, it would be satisfying if, with the help of our readings of *Iphigenia in Aulis* and *Hecuba,* we could find an answer that preserved the full force of the young girl's statement. There are indeed two precious possessions that the virgin offers up with her life, two possessions that she loses forever—the children she will never have, and the pure virginity that she is going to lose along with her life as the knife cuts her throat.

After a close reading of these texts one comes to the strange conclusion that a sacrificed virgin loses her *partheneia* (virginity) without winning a spouse. Like Iphigenia and like Polyxena, Macaria will never be a *gynē;* and yet they will not arrive in Hades as virgins. Neither woman nor virgin, but something between the two, like a *nymphē.* A *nymphē anymphos,* however, a bride without a husband. We must accept this oxymoron, applied earlier to Polyxena, as we try to understand the paradoxical image of the immolated virgin, whose *partheneia* is taken from her at the very moment when she is being exalted for the purity she shares with an untamed heifer. Our thanks must go to Macaria. As she is promised to no Achilles or Hades, Heracles' daughter forces the reader toward a bolder, or at least a more exacting, interpretation of the text. So here are some suggestions. In a general way the death of a young person in Euripidean tragedy inevitably calls forth the idea of his or her nuptials.[31] So the sacrificed virgin, the bride of Hades, is simply one embodiment of the equivalence of death and marriage. There is also, however, in Euripides a language, obscurely addressing the obscure, in which the blood-stained death of *parthenoi* is considered as an anomalous and displaced way of transforming virginity into womanhood—as though a throat-cutting equaled a defloration.[32] Iphigenia, Polyxena, and Macaria, with their throats cut, were *parthenoi aparthenoi,* virgins and yet not virgins. Under this contradictory sign, the tragic virgins of Euripides take the step that satisfies at once the anger of the gods and the dreams of the spectators.

It will certainly be objected that in Euripides, at least, there is a young sacrificial victim who is a male. He is Haemon's brother, Menoeceus, whose sacrifice to the land of Thebes is demanded, in the *Phoenissae,* by the wrath of Ares. But in Menoeceus' death one should see a masculine, because Theban, version of the sacrifice of a virgin: in the masculine world of the autochthonous *Spartoi* (the "sown men"), what victim but a male could die for the fatherland?[33] It is certainly important that the victim should be a young man and not a *parthenos.* Wielding the weapon is a man's privilege, so—as opposed to the *parthenos,* who simply succumbs to the killer's knife—the son of Creon is his own sacrificer; and in this death there is no clear distinction between sacrifice and suicide, or between suicide and a fine death in battle.[34] But it is the resemblance that is crucial rather than the difference. Menoeceus may sacrifice himself like a warrior, but it is because he is a virgin colt, still ignorant of marriage's domestication, that he is chosen as a sacrificial victim.[35] This is the moment to remind those interested in the anthropology of Greek marriage that this institution was the mark of maturity for men, too,[36] even though the transition is more marked for women. It is also, in particular, the moment to reflect on the law that makes virginity the only thing that can be fruitfully sacrificed, in order that human sacrifice, made grand by the language of tragedy, can become something fruitful for thought.

In this way Menoeceus, because he is ignorant of marriage, comes to take his place beside Iphigenia, Polyxena, and Macaria. Menoeceus acquits himself nobly, but it is still true that human sacrifice is a deviation and, when it comes to contemplating this deviation, the Greek imagination prefers to offer up a young girl to the knife. The *parthenos:* a passive and docile victim. Perhaps.

Virgin Liberty

Every animal sacrifice, to be effective, had to display the willingness of the victim.[37] A human sacrifice, even when imagined by a tragedian, could not fail to conform to this rule. The only exception would be a case in which the sacrifice was presented as pure murder, and the young girl was very far from consenting to her fate. This was the choice of Aeschylus in the *Agamemnon.*[38]

To be sure, the word *phonos* is not actually pronounced, but the virgin's immolation is clearly condemned as a defilement, impious and tainted, even before the text that describes Iphigenia being led to her fate has heaped up the charges against the father who has dared to sacrifice his child. Even the girl's status as a virgin is considered an aggravating factor ("all this, even her virginal youth, she saw go for nothing!"). But the important point is that Aeschylus leaves no room for the victim's consent, which is what gives animal sacrifice its formal legality. No sooner is the signal given for Iphigenia's throat to be cut than violence reigns. She is seized, hoisted, and gagged so that her cries should not be heard.[39] She fights back, clings to the ground, and desperately refuses her consent to this sacrifice;[40] and Aeschylus is careful to emphasize the scandal of it all.[41]

With the exception of *Iphigenia in Tauris,* in which the heroine is haunted by the dreadful memory of the violence that was done to her in a very Aeschylean style, Euripides' approach to virgin sacrifice is altogether different. He accepts the imaginary portrayal of human sacrifice only in order to distort its significance. This is a clever way of rejecting the very act that he conscientiously describes in its preparation and its performance. Under the pretense that the rule of acquiescence is being respected, consent is turned into free choice, and a death to which the victim submits becomes a willing death, not to say a noble one. Everything is in its right place, but nothing has the same meaning.

Once again Agamemnon's daughter becomes an exemplar. In *Iphigenia in Aulis* she is fully willing to die (*hekousa,* 1555). Aeschylus' Iphigenia was brutally seized and "hoisted above the altar" (*hyperthe bōmou labein aerdēn*): with an animal victim, this was a normal practice of sacrifice, but Aeschylus saw in it only a flagrant sign of violence and duress.[42] *Aerdēn,* in the air. Wives in the *aiōra* of their hanging may have freely chosen to lift themselves into the air, but the young girl who was sacrificed did not for a moment want to leave the ground. Poor Iphigenia: Euripides in *Iphigenia in Tauris* will remember all this when in the first lines of the play, in close imitation of Aeschylus' text, the daughter of Agamemnon describes the dreadful moment when, "in her misfortune seized and hoisted above the altar" (*hyper pyras metarsia lephtheisa*),[43] she was going to perish by the sword. Conversely, it is no great surprise that at the end of *Iphigenia in Aulis,* in which the liberty of the heroine would brook no constraint, even of ritual, this display of violence has disappeared. When, standing in front of her father, Iphigenia announces that she will freely surrender her body for immolation and bravely offers up her throat, by the same token she forbids the Argives to lay a finger on her—a way of refusing to be treated as a victim and "hoisted" in accordance with the ritual (*Iphigenia in Aulis* 1551–61). After this, attention is concentrated on the preparations for the immolation; on what Iphigenia was doing in these final moments (was she still proudly erect, or perhaps kneeling?) the text says no more, and the silence is eloquent. By contrast—and this is certainly not by chance—as soon as Calchas' sword has struck, the description becomes precise again—the mountain doe sacrificed in place of the young girl is stretched out on the ground with its blood spurting into the air (*ardēn*) to splash Artemis' altar.[44] With the animal victim, although it is an unorthodox one, the ritual of sacrifice resumes its course, while the *parthenos* has disappeared, leaving an unchanging image of her free choice.

However, the most complete example of this virginal refusal to be "seized and hoisted" is still Polyxena. The Greek army had expected her to fight back—a chosen band of Achaeans was given the task of controlling her desperate struggles.[45] A Trojan princess but the sister in misfortune of Iphigenia, like her immolated by the Greek army, Polyxena is able to stop the hand of the sacrificer, who is giving the signal to the chosen men to seize her (*labein*). Like

Iphigenia she proclaims her liberty, refuses to let anyone touch her, and declares that she will bare her throat courageously. From that moment, the narrative becomes more precise. Agamemnon (again!) orders the young men to let the *parthenos* go. Then the virgin Polyxena puts one knee on the ground and clings to the earth to die.[46] This bent knee is not to be taken as some barbarous oriental practice of prostration (*proskynēsis*), since Polyxena in claiming her liberty is worthy of being Greek. Still less should one think in terms of some gesture of entreaty.[47] Euripides' Polyxena, on her knees, is not begging, as she will be portrayed in later iconography, which indulges in the most sentimental interpretations of her attitude.[48] On the contrary, in that posture and the "speech of incomparable courage" that goes with it, one should see a serene acceptance of death, above all a refusal, expressed in action, to be treated as an inert body, "seized and hoisted" like Aeschylus' Iphigenia, or like the Polyxena whom, long before Euripides, the vase-painters often showed as hoisted and stretched above the altar.[49]

From the extreme constraint imposed on Aeschylus' Iphigenia (whom Euripides chose to carry away to Tauris) to the heroic liberty of Polyxena,[50] the distance is great, on a par with the reinterpretations that poets and changes of outlook have always brought to a tradition. Euripides prefers generally to grant the *parthenos* the courage and free choice that, in the untragic conditions of real life, were denied to the young Greek girl by society. Courage and decision were also the hallmarks of Macaria's character, together with her repeated affirmation of liberty. She too did not want to die at men's hands, but the text of the *Heraclidae,* strangely, refuses her the posthumous tribute of describing her death.[51]

Macaria, Polyxena, Iphigenia. They are freed from their fathers in the moment when their fathers condemn them to immolation; they turn to their own use the freedom of choice that characterized the *kyrios*,[52] by taking over the sacrifice imposed on them and turning it into *their* death, a death that is fully their own.

Their deaths are fully their own, and claimed as such: some commentators promptly classify them as suicides.[53] In doing this they reduce the significance of the bold departure by which the sacrificial victim gains control over her own death. Does a voluntary sacrifice belong with suicide? It would be better to see in it a variant on the "fine death" that is accepted for country or for glory—a very peculiar variant, since the death is a virgin's. The very word *hekousa* ("of my own free will") used by the chosen *parthenoi* to express this unforced consent to sacrifice is very like the rhetorical formula (*ethelein apothnēiskein*) that expresses the acceptance of death by the citizen. For the noble death is not sought after, but accepted. Just as the Athenians or Spartans bow before a demand laid upon them by their city, so the virgins accept a destiny that they reclaim as their own.[54]

But of course nothing is that simple in Euripides, and in this subtle merging of sacrifice and noble death, suicide sometimes has a place. Take the case of the death of Erechtheus' daughters. In the *Ion,* except for Creusa, who was spared because of her youth (277–278), these *parthenoi* were *sphagia,* sacrificial victims whom their father "dared to immolate for the soil of Athens." There is every sign in the *Erechtheus* that only one of the girls was sacrificed, or rather that she died a noble death in the sacrifice. For the command given by Athena at the end of the play "to bury her exactly where [*houper*] she died" is identical to the privilege accorded by the Athenians to their fellow citizen Tellus, when they buried him "exactly where he had fallen"[55] for his country. Up to this point, everything seems clear. Too clear perhaps, for Athena goes on to order Praxithea, wife of the king and mother of the young girl, to bury the victim's sisters in the same tomb, those sisters who in loyalty to their oath had killed themselves over the body of the slaughtered virgin. So it comes about that a common tomb—an honor usually reserved for warriors, "whose glory is evenly shared"—will house the bodies of virgins and, what is more, will reunite in death the sacrificial victim and the young suicides.[56] The goddess justifies these funeral honors by the nobility (*gennaiotēs*) shown by the sisters, and presents their suicide as a virginal form of heroic death. Thus sacrifice, suicide, and noble death exist side by side and overlap. But when one is dealing with a tragedy of Euripides, who would expect one unambiguous reading? The confusion of genres, institutions, and languages is very typical of Euripides in practice, whatever his "intentions" may have been—whether he was being ironical or not, whether he did or did not mean to expose to the judgment of the spectators these armies of men who find their salvation in the blood of virgins.[57]

The Glory of Young Girls

So, to the *parthenoi* a noble death and glory forever.

Death, for young girls and mature women alike, was bound up with marriage and glory, but there is no doubt that the renown of virgins resembled the *eukleia* (glory) of warriors more than the renown of wives did.

Glory indeed is essentially virile, and to Menoeceus, the "young colt" who died a soldier's death, the epithet "victorious" was given without question. But the *parthenos* Cassandra in Aeschylus was also victorious, in agreeing to a bloody death that would launch the cycle of murders and so avenge her fallen family.[58] The Antigone of Sophocles was glorious in her *hybris,* the only mortal to go down to the land of the dead of her own free will (*autonomos*).[59] As for the sacrificed virgins, enough has been said to show that glory was bestowed on them without reserve. Macaria had glory, and Polyxena, and so did Iphigenia at Aulis, for whom the chorus women would sing a paean,[60] as though virile grandeur left the male side and moved to these girls whose virginity was taken with their lives. In her sudden resolve, which has astonished more than one commentator, the daughter of Agamemnon, the paradigmatic *parthenos,* won for herself and for her sisters in glorious misfortune an excellence (*aretē*) greater than that of Achilles.[61]

Thus, around the sacrifice of virgins, tragedy develops a reflection on the problematic condition of the *parthenos.* This reflection subverts the processes of marriage by looking at them through the prism of sacrificial rites and showing how little, in many respects, they are distorted by that; but it also creates, within the limits of an imaginative construction, a version of glory that is peculiarly virginal. As a goddess Artemis can well identify with her title *Eukleia,* for she is the "Glorious One." But what can be said about the glory of those mortal girls who die for it, except that it is stolen, as it were, from the warriors who will not die since virgin's blood has flowed on their behalf? Within the imaginary world of tragedy, there still remains an impossibility through which reality reclaims its rights: when young girls die, or when, as we have seen, wives die, there are no words available to denote the glory of a woman that do not belong to the language of male renown.[62]

And glory always makes the blood of women flow.[63]

· III ·

Regions of the Body

THERE are, after all, benefits to be had from the world of the imagination. The woman in tragedy is better served than the ordinary wife and the young girl, departed before their time, who appear in epitaphs—pale wraiths of discourse whose beauty is never mentioned. The woman in tragedy, in the interplay of glory and death, acquires a body. It is, to be sure, a body through which death will come to her—but, with the imaginary, the rule of the game is that what you win you instantly lose.

There is a body, then; but it is poorly known. An anthropological approach to tragedy is generally more concerned with institutional practices than with corporeal schemata, and it has not always paid enough attention to this topography of the body, which in tragedy, from Aeschylus to Euripides, is structured around the places of death. To end this study, I should like to try to draw up a list of those places through which death comes to women. It must come from a word-by-word study of the texts, for here, again, one has to back the precision of the signifier in tragedy. This precision is determinedly clinical: thus, contrary to what may be suggested by translators who are keener to transpose the texts than to leave them with the specific sense of the Greek, the "liver" in tragedy is indeed always the liver, and not something like the heart.[1] It is not trivial that when Deianira is pierced to the liver, death comes to her in the same way that it comes to men. But let us not anticipate.

Women's Weak Point

Creon and his men were horrified by the sudden sight—brutal and irrevocable—of Antigone's corpse "hanged by the neck," *kremastēn auchenos* (Sophocles, *Antigone* 1221). But the word most used by Euripides to describe those hapless women, hanging with their neck in a noose, is *derē*.[2] A richer word, no doubt, because it carries a much stronger affective charge. What the daughter of Oedipus, silent and abandoned, has imprisoned in the knot of her veil, *auchēn*, is the neck seen from the nape. *Derē*, on the contrary, is "the front of the neck, the throat," a strong point of feminine beauty—whether one thinks of the "splendid throat" of Aphrodite by which, in the third book of the *Iliad*, Helen recognizes the goddess; or the "delicate throat" that Sappho's lover delighted in covering with flowers; or again the "neck of startling whiteness" that Medea, under her nurse's gaze, turns to hide her tears. But *derē* is also what, in an ecstasy of mourning, virgins and women delight in tearing, sharp nail on soft throat.[3]

Derē is all these things, and, for a woman, it is above all the point of greatest vulnerability. It is by that part that one hangs, and by that part also that death comes to young girls chosen for sacrifice. For in accounts of immolation *derē* means the exact spot where the officiating priests apply the knife at the moment of execution.[4] So Iphigenia remembers in Tauris: "Ah, when my poor father brought his sword near to my throat . . ." So Achilles warns the daughter of Agamemnon: "When you see the sword very near to your throat . . ." Iphigenia's throat, the throat of Polyxena covered in gold, which will soon be stained purple with blood.

There is no point in multiplying examples of *derē* in a sacrificial context.[5] All that one need say is that, where there is *derē*, there is still breath and life. At this word, more than once, the description of an immolation pauses as the menace is for a moment held back, and the virgin, with the knife at her throat, still breathes. But where a throat has already been cut or is being penetrated by the sword, *derē* gives way to *laimos*, the word for the throat considered as the gullet;[6] for once the fair surface of the neck has been pierced, death starts to slip into the interior of the body. So the language of tragedy is again, as always, precise, and so too are the descriptions. At the moment of striking Iphigenia, the priest examines the throat (*laimos*) of the victim with the sharp eye of an anatomist, to pick out the point where the knife will sink in best (*Iphigenia in Aulis* 1579). In the *Orestes,* just as he thinks he can at last slay Helen as an expiatory victim, the hero forces her neck (*derē*) against her left shoulder and prepares to "drive his black sword into her throat [*laimos*]." More than one commentator has rightly recognized in this the exact picture of a sacrificer in action.[7]

All, then, is in order—the order prescribed for a killing. However, there may also be, hidden away, some secret order that governs the female body. It is as though, quite apart from ritual practice and its requirements, the throats of women invited death: to kill Clytemnestra, Orestes strikes her in the throat—a way no doubt for Euripides to make a comment on the word *sphagē*.[8] It is through the neck (*dia mesou auchenos*) that Jocasta in the *Phoenissae* sinks her sword as she kills herself (1457). If we recall that the Jocasta of Sophocles, more conventionally, put her neck in a noose, we can see in this detail a hint from Euripides, who is deliberately emphasizing the way in which the heroine's soldierlike suicide departs from a well-established tradition.

Similarly, with regard to the cutting of Clytemnestra's throat, one may call to mind again the lying speech in the *Agamemnon* in which she maintains that she has more than once passed a rope round her neck (*derē*, 875). Jocasta, Clytemnestra—two ways for a woman to be killed, at the place where she ought to have tied a noose. In each case, someone will invoke overdetermination. But it is a remarkable overdetermination that, whether it be hanging or *sphagē*, suicide,[9] murder, or sacrifice, requires women to die by the throat, and only by the throat.

At this point the reader will no doubt ask what happens in tragedy with the death of men. The answer is that in fact they seldom die from being struck in the throat, whether they are murdered or fall in battle.[10] If Clytemnestra's death is meant to avenge Agamemnon's "by the same ways" (*tropōn tōn autōn*), it is a reference to parricide that should be heard in this expression, not to the exact method of the murder. For if we are to believe Sophocles, the betrayed king was struck down by the blow of an ax full on the brow.[11] In Homer the neck is one of the warrior's most vulnerable points, for it is there, *di' auchenos,* that Achilles drives his javelin into Hector's body, and in the *Iliad* there are many warriors who die with their throats cut.[12] But there is nothing of this sort to be found in the world of tragedy. The most we can do is to quote a chorus of the *Phoenissae* on the single combat of the two sons of Oedipus, which will make "the blood flow from the brother's throat [*homogenē deran*]."[13] However, apart from the fact that death came to Eteocles and Polynices by quite other means, it will be readily agreed that the duel of two brothers, the ultimate expression of a civil war at the family level, partakes more of *sphagē* than of war.

There is a conclusion of this analysis that we cannot avoid: death lurks in the throats of women, hidden in their beauty, which the texts never evoke more freely than at the precise moment when their lives are threatened and in the balance. White throat of the grief-stricken Medea, whose nurse fears she may kill herself; the perfect white neck of Iphigenia, over whom the murderous sword is already standing guard.[14] The Euripidean fantasy of the knife on the throat reveals tragedy's concept of feminine seduction, which is especially dangerous for the woman who is its too vulnerable agent.

A Recital of the Male Body

In epic there is no point in the body through which death is not able to "tame" the male. There is the neck, of course, but also the belly (*Iliad* XI.381), the forehead, the temple, the side, the right breast, the chest and the lung, the groin, the navel, the heel. There I shall stop the recital; its only point is to suggest the richness of the male body in Homer, which is vulnerable all over to tearing, slicing, and felling.[15] Tragedy certainly does not take over this compulsive list, but it does still endow the male with a body that is infinitely more diversified than that of a woman, so far as ways of access for death are concerned.

There is the side (*pleuron*), which the warrior protects in battle all the more carefully because he dies if he is pierced there;[16] and murder, too, seems to make its fatal way into man's body in this region. Thus, Neoptolemus, treacherously set upon in Delphi and struck by a hail of missiles, falls only when a sharp sword wounds him in the side.[17] There is the stomach, where Polynices in the *Phoenissae* is mortally struck by a blow on the navel; and there is the whole cavity within the body, where even physicians do not always clearly distinguish higher and lower, or front and side, because everything is so interconnected that a mortal blow can be said to sink in "through the lungs" or "through the side."[18] In the same area of the body, the blow to the liver is especially fatal for the warrior—the wound which in the *Erechtheus* brings about the death of Eumolpus, and which, in the *Phoenissae,* Polynices on the point of death manages to inflict on Eteocles. This is a mortal blow above all others, since Eteocles dies before his brother, unable to utter one more word; it is a deadly blow whose devastating power was well known to the enchantress Medea, who, in her plan for a triple murder that was to look like an engagement of war, dreamed for a while of striking the king of Corinth, his daughter, and Jason in the liver.[19]

So the side and the liver are two fatal places on a warrior's body. It is there that a man sinks in his sword to commit suicide. In the side, like Haemon or like Ajax, that paradigm of the manly suicide:[20] in the liver, the method that Heracles, Orestes, or Menelaus imagined, when they thought of destroying themselves, just long enough to underline the nobility attaching to such a death.[21] In fact the liver is a vital organ (which does not warrant its being systematically translated as "the heart" where the Greek says *hēpar*), and the "blow in the liver" is the metaphor most used in tragedy to express the violence of an emotion.[22]

To come back to those blows that are not in the least metaphorical, real blows that open up the body to death. They are the blows that men sustain, but, all the same, there are women in tragedy who die of them. The suicide by a blow to the liver that in Euripides is contemplated by such heroes as Heracles, Orestes, or Electra (*Electra* 688)—this is something that in Sophocles some women, in their despair, find the courage to carry through. I have in mind Eurydice, whose death, at once sacrificial and like that of a warrior,[23] dealt a final blow ot Creon's doubtful manliness. Above all I have in mind Deianira, that fragile wife who knew only too well how death comes to warriors, for without hesitation she pierced her side "with a two-edged dagger, rammed home between the liver and the diaphragm" (*Trachiniae* 930–931).

However, it is not self-evident that a woman could carry through to the end a man's death: she could not, for instance, force language to invent a feminine form for military terms such as *parastatēs* (companion in the ranks), which occur only in the masculine.[24] So we should scrutinize more closely this form of suicide "that a hand of woman has dared carry out" (*Trachiniae* 898). No doubt it was a manly death[25] achieved in the Homeric style by the "groaning steel that slices the flesh" (*Trachiniae* 886–887). And indeed, to kill herself, Deianira uncovered those martial parts of the body—the side and the arm.[26] But this is just where the difficulty starts. To strike herself below the liver, Deianira uncovered her *left* side (*Trachiniae* 931) and not her right side, as one would expect, even if one's anatomical knowledge were minimal. Commentators are bewildered and ask whether Sophocles may have been careless. A lazy explanation, and so the least satisfactory.[27] It would be better to follow Jebb's commentary with its suggestion that in this case Sophocles uses the word *hēpar* in the very general sense of the "center of life." However, such a use would not justify putting the organ in its wrong place, and besides, one would still have to explain why Deianira strikes on the left side—a detail which is puzzling but which cannot possibly have been added randomly. I take another view and submit that this anomaly is pregnant with meaning; for in exposing her left flank the wife of Heracles laid bare the female side.[28] It is a textual ruse, a contradiction deliberately presented to emphasize that a woman's death, even if contrived in the most manly way, does not escape the laws of her sex.

So we have to sustain an inconsistency that is full of meaning. Deianira did indeed die from a blow under the liver *and* on her left, as a woman in love who wanted *in extremis* to assume the values of the martial world.[29] We can take it that a man's body, even when viewed through the ambiguity of tragedy, would not show such inconsistencies.

Polyxena's Alternative

Here is another anomaly, an ever so slight one—or rather a question. Why does Polyxena, on the point of being sacrificed and having just declared herself ready "to proffer the neck [*derēn*] of a valiant spirit" (Euripides, *Hecuba* 549), change her mind and give Neoptolemus the choice between two ways of killing her?

It is true that in the meantime the head of the Achaean army has given the "chosen" an order to release the young girl. Whereupon Polyxena, making the best of the liberty that remains to her, takes the initiative:

> When she had heard the masters' words, she seized her veils and tore them from the shoulder down to the middle of her side near where the navel is, uncovering her breasts and her bosom as lovely as that of a statue [*mastous t'*... *sterna th' hōs agalmatos kallista*]. Then, placing one knee on the ground, she uttered these words of incomparable gallantry: "Here is my bosom [*sternon*], young man. Strike there, if that is where you would like to strike. If you would prefer the neck [*hyp' auchena*], here is my throat [*laimos*] ready." (*Hecuba* 557–565)

Neoptolemus hesitates. But it is not the alternative offered by Polyxena that makes him "wish and not wish"; it is simply "pity for the young girl." Without further hesitation and like a skilled sacrificer "he cuts her windpipe with the steel."[30] That is to say, he chooses the normal way. No sacrificer would strike in the chest, and there are very few women in tragedy to whom death comes through the breast.[31] So what did Polyxena mean when she spoke to Neoptolemus in this way?

In Aristotle's language, this problem would not arise, since, by his anatomical criteria, *sphagē,* the word for a throat virtually opened up, is used to indicate precisely "the part common to the neck and to the breast."[32] However, in the tragic universe in which Polyxena dies, no compromise can eliminate the choice between these two, and the regions of the body carry such strong symbolic values that any choice between them—certainly where tradition did not impose one—has a definite meaning.

Sternon or *laimos?* Since the "bosom" is topographically opposed to the severed throat, we should, like Euripides, consider the naked beauty of Polyxena. Perhaps it is not the nudity of the *parthenos* in itself that should claim our attention. Virgins being sacrificed are usually stripped of their clothes,[33] and, as she means to be free to the end, Polyxena herself does what *parthenoi* who are being sacrificed are forced to undergo.[34] But Polyxena's nakedness, described in its beauty as like a statue, stared at by the Achaean army, is treated by Euripides as a spectacle—as it will remain, from Hellenistic painting up to the art of Pietro da Cortona.[35] Polyxena uncovered her breasts (*mastous*) and her fine bosom (*sterna*). This conjunction is not a pleonasm; the two words carry such different meanings that Euripides rarely uses them together. A good example of a "partial object," *mastos* is the mother's breast swollen with milk, but it is also, fleetingly glimpsed, the erotically provocative bosom of the beautiful Helen, at the sight of which Menelaus one day dropped his sword,[36] as the Greeks loved to recount. The values of the *sternon* are more diverse. In a man the "chest" is a region of the body that is thought a particularly good place to strike an enemy in battle: he is killed at a blow and, not having run away, earns a noble death.[37] The woman's bosom is mainly conjured up as a source of affect, aesthetic or sentimental: *sternon* of Electra or Iphigenia, clasped in the tender embrace of Orestes or Agamemnon; tender bosom of the virgin Iphigenia, which Agamemnon, weeping over the beauty of his sacrificial victim, evokes together with the virgin's lovely cheeks and her fair hair; and the white bosom that women uncover as they mourn, to strike it or tear it, in a contrast that is very telling.[38]

By associating these two words, mentioning the desirable breast at the same time as the shapely bosom,[39] does the description of Polyxena in her nakedness merely aim to eroticize the virgin's death? Again a distinction must be made between what the army sees (of which the messenger's speech professes to be a faithful testimony) and what Polyxena wants. The choice she proposes to Neoptolemus is an initiative of the *parthenos* and has meaning for her alone. In fact, as she addresses Achilles' son, Polyxena does not talk of those desirable breasts on which the Greek army feasted their eyes, but only of her *sternon:* "Here is my bosom, young man. If it is there that you prefer to strike, strike there." So Polyxena does not speak out in order to eroticize her end; her only ambition in Hades is to lie dead among the dead, and, as she dies, she is able to show a modesty of the most virginal kind.[40] So what is it, then, that gives meaning to her proposal?

If we are reluctant to press the interpretation further and prefer to stop at this question, we may make some progress by turning to Roman accounts of Polyxena's death, if only because they show that, despite a range of variations, Euripides was always read in the same way, one that places the young girl's end in the context of martial courage.

Take Seneca's Polyxena, who is to marry Achilles in death and whose immolation matches, in considerable detail, a marriage ceremony.[41] Then, at the moment of death, to the amazement of the reader looking for a "nuptial sacrifice,"[42] the virgin (*virgo*) becomes a *virago,* and the tender victim behaves like a fighter meeting a fatal blow head on: "Far from withdrawing, the courageous and manly young girl [*audax virago*] turned toward the fatal blow, drawing herself up proudly and showing no fear." And the crowd admires her courage (*tam fortis animus*) (Seneca, *Troades* 1151–53). Seneca is a good reader of Euripides. Could this be a way of commenting on Polyxena's proposal ("If you prefer to strike me in the breast, strike there")?

Without rushing to conclusions we can turn to Ovid, an even more faithful reader of Euripides. In book XIII of the *Metamorphoses,* Polyxena, "unhappy virgin raised by her courage above her sex" (*plus quam femina virgo*), is led to the tomb of Achilles, to have her throat cut. The daughter of Priam talks to the hero's son in the same language as in Greek tragedy ("Plunge your weapon into my throat or my bosom," *jugulo vel pectore*), and, at the same moment, she uncovers her throat and her bosom. As in Euripides, she falls "taking care to veil those parts of her body that she wishes to hide from the general view, and to observe the decencies that modesty imposes on a chaste woman."[43] Ovid, however, in choosing where to deal the mortal blow, gave the sacrificer the action that Euripides did not allow Neoptolemus: "The officiant, himself weeping, sadly plunges the steel into the bosom that is offered to his blows" (*Metamorphoses* XIII.475–476).

This difference, all the more remarkable because what

leads up to it is so faithful to the Greek model, needs explaining. Perhaps one can call on some taste for this kind of death, peculiar to Ovid[44] or Latin poetry. We will remember no doubt that Camilla in the *Aeneid* was mortally wounded in her naked breast.[45] However, when one sees that Ovid, in what follows, insistently comments on the courage of Polyxena, fallen, like her brothers, to Achilles' sword (*Metamorphoses* XIII.497–500), one becomes convinced that there is more to be said. So I would suggest that in choosing to let the virgin have the death that in Euripides she suggested she might have, the Latin poet meant to outdo Euripides by giving its fullest meaning to the alternative that Euripides introduced: in the throat, like a sacrificial victim, or in the breast, like a warrior.

We have now formulated the interpretation at which we hesitated earlier. The Greek army may have been dazzled by the feminine attractions of Polyxena's nakedness, but for the *parthenos* the blow in the breast simply meant that Neoptolemus was paying a proper tribute to her *andreia*. But *andreia,* of course, the name of courage, refers to a male virtue . . . So the detour we have made through Latin poetry will have served to confirm *a contrario* a proposition we were already in a position to support when discussing Deianira: whatever freedom the tragic discourse of the Greeks offered to women, it did not allow them ultimately to transgress the frontier that divided and opposed the sexes. Tragedy certainly does transgress and mix things up—this is its rule, its nature—but never to the point of irrevocably overturning the civic order of values; a "manly woman" has to be menacing and not seductive, something that Clytemnestra can be, and Polyxena cannot. Polyxena could indeed offer up her bosom like a warrior, but the Greek army saw in the gesture only a virgin unveiling her woman's breasts.

It is at the throat, therefore, that in Euripides Neoptolemus, as a good sacrificer, slaughters the virgin; she is struck at women's weak point[46] and is reclaimed at the last moment by femininity. Doubtless it was not in tragedy's power to upset a well-established discourse. Wasn't it again in the throat, or, if you prefer, the neck that in archaic times Achilles dealt Penthesilea a mortal blow?[47] It is always the throat, in war as in sacrifice, and that choice is certainly significant, in a tradition fed by epic, in which the whole of a man's body is laid open to fatal wounds. To cast light on the regularity—one might almost say, the monotony—of this pattern, one should look for a principle outside the universe of tragedy and move toward the gynecological thinking of the Greeks, where woman is caught between two mouths, between two necks,[48] where vagaries of the womb suddenly choke the voice in a woman's throat,[49] and where many a young girl old enough to be a *nymphē* hangs herself to escape the threat of the terrifying suffocation inside her body.[50] Anyone at all familiar with Freud's work will remember Dora, the cough that was one of her symptoms, and the remarks of Freud on "this displacement from the lower to the upper part of the body," which invades the throat because "that part of the body had to a high degree retained its significance as an erogenous zone in the young girl."[51] However, once one immerses oneself in the medical thought of the Greeks, or joins up, bag and baggage, with psychoanalysis,[52] one can find no way of rejoining the tragic universe. For tragedy wants no part of this gynecological imagery, or at least does not want to talk of it explicitly. It is enough to note this silence without pressing it, and to suggest that in the tragic body nothing is left to the whims of free association, because in it all the places of death have their proper locations.

INNOVATION, orthodoxy; liberty, constraint: it was against the background of this tension that women's destiny was played out in tragedy, as no doubt it was at many levels of civic experience in Athens. But there is this special feature of tragedy, that because it notably exalts the role of liberty, the effect of constraint in it—however subtle it may be, however covertly present in this or that signifier—is all the more powerful because it shows up in words rather than in institutions. There is this feature, too, that innovation takes place in the purely verbal context of fiction, and the royal road to it is death.[53]

To interest oneself in what is said about women's deaths in tragedy is to enjoy a privileged viewpoint. It is true that once the firm line has been drawn separating feminine from masculine, Greek creative imagination delights in blurring it; but where is the best place to try to define the processes and limits of the game, if not at the institutional center of this confusion, right inside the space in which tragedy produces its interference?[54]

This has been my plan. The aim was to determine how and to what extent manly values and feminine attributes acted on one another in the tragic presentation of women, because, where this shadowy "half of the city's population" is concerned, tragedy can be readily credited with a boldness remarkable in fifth-century Athens. The fact that this boldness turns out to be less than one had supposed is not disquieting in itself. Any investigation runs the risk, as it proceeds, of challenging or modifying the initial hypotheses, especially when these were adopted with only one preconception—that at all costs the sterile opposition between feminism and misogyny should be avoided. I have simply done my best to follow the twists and turns of tragedy's very unusual orthodoxy. It has given me pleasure—the pleasure that comes from exploring byways—

and it has been perhaps not without profit. This meandering journey at least provides an opportunity to ask clearer questions about the important deviations that may exist within an established genre. Such in fact is the paradox of women's glorious death—for death to be noble it must be manly. Therefore, wives and young girls, if they are going to win the elusive *kleos gynaikōn*, must strive for *andreia*. It is precisely at this point that femininity is on the watch and pulls them back, without their knowledge, but to the great edification of the audience: it happens in an instant, in the time taken by one word that represents a deeply significant choice made by the tragic text. In this respect Euripides, whether he was in fact an admirer or an enemy of women (tradition has never really been able to decide on this point), is the equal of Sophocles, that master of ambiguity. This all goes to show that tragedy displays virtually an unchanging tendency to think of femininity in the same terms.

This is indeed a very general conclusion to reach after a long spell of reading, in which word-for-word attention has deliberately been paid to the texts. Yet such a generalization reveals the true benefit of an inquiry of this sort. Indeed, in speaking generally of "deaths of women in tragedy," I was already aiming at a generalization, taking a chance on the genre as such. To take a chance on the genre commits one to assuming that it has a unity, or at least to trying to discover its constants. These constants can be defined as shared aspects of tragic discourse—shared even when, from one author to another, they are fiercely contested. If this was to be my aim, it immediately followed that I could not accept either of two well-established ways of reading the tragedians. One of these is founded on the sacrosanct dogma of evolution, which decrees that from Aeschylus to Sophocles and from Sophocles to Euripides (even though the last two were more or less contemporary) the notions and intellectual choices change and, as the theory has it, evolve. The other way wants to isolate each body of work in its own particular nature and is intent on extracting each tragic writer's predilection for some particular motif: Aeschylus is obviously very interested in the violence of murder, Sophocles in the desperate will that drives someone on to suicide, Euripides in the immolation of tender virgins.[55] These are well-marked paths, and, without neglecting them, I have preferred to make a different journey. It matters to me, in closing, that it should be agreed that the route was a sound one; in other words, it should be agreed that, granted all the differences, the interrogation of femininity goes on in much the same terms from one tragedian to another (as with this verb *aeirō*, to which, contrary to what one might expect, we have come back several times), and also within the same limits (represented, for instance, by the idea that a woman's throat tends to enclose her death).

To bring out these very overdetermined elements of discourse, there is now a well-marked way that consists in submitting the texts of tragedy to questions put by an anthropology of the ancient world. This is a fruitful approach, as has been amply shown, but only on condition that it is coupled with a tireless attention to the special nature of the particular genre. So I have tried to open out the questions of anthropology into an inquiry more closely centered on the directions and the forms taken by the imagination among the Greeks, in order to understand what kind of benefit accrued to the city through this event institutionally separated from the rest of its life, the dramatic performance. Put another way, how far is the oxymoron, so dear to tragic texts, essential to the representations that the city gives of itself in drama? Or again, what do spectators in the theater gain from thinking, in the mode of fiction, things that in everyday life cannot and must not be thought? It is a

chance, then, to reflect on the aim of the tragic "purifi-
cation,"[56] which surely purges the citizen more than the
private individual, because it purges emotions that should
be unknown to the ideal of a good citizen. So virgins are
sacrificed in the theater of Dionysus . . .

In trying to search out the ways in which the city's
thought worked, I have concentrated on the signifier, which
is like a subtext to the text of the tragedians and can, perhaps, be identified only through reading. This has meant
that I have moved back to a point that comes well before
any achieved tragic effect, toward the margins of what
makes the genre intelligible at all. So I have willingly taken
up the rather prosaic role of reader. We have to reconcile
ourselves to the fact that we shall never be in the position of
the spectators in fifth-century Athens. But all the same, we
can see clearly enough—I rest my hopes on this—to understand what it was in the death of Deianira or the sacrifice of
Polyxena that gave the Athenian spectator the controlled
pleasure afforded by an enjoyment of the deviant when it is
acted out, reflected upon, and tamed.

Notes

Cast of Characters

Index

NOTES

Preface

1. Aristotle, *Poetics* 1452b11–13. Unless otherwise indicated, all translations are my own.

2. This is how H. C. Baldry (*The Greek Tragic Theatre,* London, 1971, pp. 50–51) describes tragedy's preference for the text.

3. I borrow this term from J.-P. Vernant, "Tensions and Ambiguities in Greek Tragedy," in *Tragedy and Myth in Ancient Greece,* ed. J.-P. Vernant and P. Vidal-Naquet (Hassocks: Harvester Press, 1981), p. 17.

4. Ibid., p. 18.

5. Except for miming certain words, to supplement the very inadequate attention paid by the modern spectator to long discursive passages. Thus in Jean-Phillipe Guerlais's recent staging of the *Oresteia* in Paris (Orbe Theatre, 1984), the actual brandishing of the doe, hare, and eagles in the first chorus of the *Agamemnon* amounted to suggesting the violent realism of the textual signifier. This policy should be distinguished from the practice of "acting" the text, which is open to the dangers of psychologizing.

6. What Roland Barthes, talking about Racinian tragedy, called "great masses of solid language" (*Sur Racine,* Paris: Le Seuil, 1963, p. 21).

7. "Which is the only tragic order," again said Barthes, reflecting on Racinian "decorum" (ibid., pp. 17–18).

8. I am using for my own ends an expression used by Marie Moscovici in connection with Freud's work on the words of everyday speech, whose "sexual consistency he has discovered" but from which he has made "words that somehow are in the know" ("La déclaration," *L'Ecrit du Temps,* 1 [1982], 209).

9. See pp. 20, 42–44.

10. One sign among others that there are pitfalls in working on the difference between the sexes. When I gave this title to the third part of my book, I had quite "forgotten" that this was the title of issue 3 of the *Nouvelle Revue de Psychanalyse* in spring 1971.

Introduction

1. W. Peek, *Griechische Vers-Inschriften* (Berlin: Berlin Akad. Verlag, 1955), no. 1491: Athens, fourth century B.C.

2. Thucydides II.45.2, a remark that has been commented on and discussed ad infinitum, starting with Plutarch, who, at the beginning of *De mulierum virtutibus*, attacks such an idea. But Plutarch, who sees in feminine virtues "a good deal of historical exposition," belongs to an era in which the literary genres were less centered on the city than in classical times, and so there was room for women's participation in history.

3. Herodotus II.89 (the corpses of beautiful Egyptian women); II.1 (Cassandane), 129 (the daughter of Mycerinus); III.31–32 (the sister/wife of Cambyses); IV.205 (Pheretima).

4. Euripides (*Hippolytus* 813) calls the hanging of Phaedra a *biaios thanatos* (violent death).

5. *Oedipus Tyrannus* 1230: *hekonta kouk akonta*. See also 1237: *autē pros hautēs*. In contrast to Deianira or Eurydice, whose deaths were attributed to an outside responsibility (*aitia*), the *aitia* of Jocasta's death was entirely laid at her door. The quotation that follows is found at 1234–35.

6. See Sophocles, *Trachiniae* 878 and 880, *Antigone* 1174; Euripides, *Hippolytus* 801, *Phoenissae* 1354.

I. The Rope and the Sword

1. Compare Euripides, *Medea* 39–40 and 379.

2. The knot of the rope (*brochos*) makes real the metaphorical knot of misfortune. Compare *Hippolytus* 671 and 781.

3. A. Katsouris ("The Suicide Motive in Ancient Drama," *Dioniso,* 47 [1956], 5–36) asserts this, although he cannot avoid admitting (p. 9) that in tragedy the majority of suicides were committed by women.

4. It is worth remembering that traditionally Ajax is the only male hero to carry a suicide through to the end. The interpretation of Heracles' choice proposed here contradicts that of Jacqueline de Romilly ("Le refus du suicide dans l'Héraclès d'Euripide," *Arkhaiognosia,* 1 [1980], 1–10.

5. This shows all the difference between a wish of reason (*ethelō*) and an inclination (*boulomai*). See Nicole Loraux, *The Invention of Athens* (Cambridge, Mass.: Harvard University Press, 1986), pp. 102–104, and, on Aristodamus (Herodotus IX.71), "La belle mort spartiate," *Ktema,* 2 (1977), 105–120. It should be noted that, in *Le suicide* (new ed., Paris: Presses Universitaires de France, 1981, p. 374), Emile Durkheim inter-

prets Aristodamus' death as a suicide. Othryadas: Herodotus I.82; Pantites: Herodotus VII.232.

6. For example, *autophonos* and *autocheir*. The overdetermination suicide/death in combat/family murder is particularly clear in the single combat between the sons of Oedipus. See Aeschylus, *Seven against Thebes* 850; Sophocles, *Antigone* 172; Euripides, *Phoenissae* 880. Other examples are Aeschylus, *Agamemnon* 1091; Euripides, *Orestes* 947; and Sophocles, *Antigone* 1175. See also the commentary of L. Gernet on book IX of Plato's *Laws* (Paris: Ernest Leroux, 1917), p. 162 (873c5–6).

7. This is one of the extenuating circumstances envisaged by Plato in his condemnation of suicide (*Laws* IX.873c5–6).

8. Shame: Plato, *Laws* IX.873e6; ugliness of hanging: Euripides, *Helen* 298–302; defilement: Sophocles, *Antigone* 54 (*lōbē*), also Aeschylus, *Supplices* 473 (*miasma* in a system of suicide as revenge); dishonor: Euripides, *Helen* 134–136, 200–202, 686–687 (death of Leda).

9. As it closes forever the too open bodies of women, hanging is almost latent in feminine physiology. See Nicole Loraux, "Le corps étranglé," in *Le châtiment dans la cité*, ed. Y. Thomas (Rome and Paris: Ecole Française de Rome, 1984), pp. 195–218.

10. Sophocles, *Antigone* 1220–22; Aeschylus, *Supplices* 455–466.

11. Poison: *Agamemnon* 1260–63. The veil as net: ibid., 1382–83, 1492, 1580, 1611; *Choephoroe* 981–982, 998–1004; *Eumenides* 460, 634–635. Deianira: Sophocles, *Trachiniae* 883–884 (*emēsato*), 928 (*technomenēs*). The mixing of the "straight path" of the sword and of *mētis* is at its height in *Medea* 384–409 and 1278 (where the sword is a net).

12. Hanging rather than the male: Aeschylus, *Supplices* 787–790; precipitation rather than the *daiktōr*: 794–799. Compare *daiktōr* with *gōos daiktēr*, *Seven against Thebes* 917: a tearing sob, a doleful mourning in which one tears one's body in imitation of the torn bodies of the dead, in this case the sons of Oedipus, themselves *autodaiktoi*, 735. Finally, note that at line 680 of the *Supplices*, the verb *daizō* (tear) has made its first appearance, to characterize civil war as the tearer of the city. So there is no reason to turn "tearer" euphemistically into "ravisher."

13. Euripides, *Alcestis* 74–76. Other metaphors of death as cutting or bloody: 118 and 225. On Thanatos as the masculine form of death, see J.-P. Vernant, "Figures féminines de la mort," forthcoming in a collective work *Masculin/Féminin en Grèce ancienne* (ed. Nicole Loraux).

14. Euripides, *Andromache* 616: *oude trōtheis*. It is the scholiast who is right (as opposed to L. Méridier, the translator of the Belles Lettres edition). Menelaus in book IV of the *Iliad* was certainly wounded from

afar by an arrow from Pandarus, but no wound was inflicted on him at close quarters, by a sword or a lance; and this was the sign of his dubious courage.

15. Euripides, *Iphigenia in Tauris* 621–622. On the place given to the slaughterer at the heart of feminine sacrifice, see M. Detienne, "Violentes Eugénies," in *La cuisine du sacrifice en pays grec,* ed. M. Detienne and J.-P. Vernant (Paris: Gallimard, 1979), p. 208.

16. On this exchange, on which I have commented in "Blessures de virilité" (*Le Genre Humain,* 10 [1984], 38–56), see Pindar, *Nemean* VIII.40 (also *Nemean* VII.35 and *Isthmian* IV.35). We must remember that in the tragedy of Sophocles, Hector's sword is a gift from the enemy. As for Ajax, he dies as a warrior "falls" (*piptō: Ajax* 828, 841, 1033).

17. *Ajax* 815, with the translation and commentary of J. Casabona, *Recherches sur le vocabulaire des sacrifices en Grèce* (Aix-en-Provence: Annales Fac. Lettres, 1966), p. 179. One will note that the sword is set upright (*hestēken*) as is usually a hoplite at his post. In 1026 Teucer speaks of his sword as a *phoneus,* a killer.

18. The blade: *Ajax* 581–582, in a context at once medical and sacrificial (cf. *Trachiniae* 1032–33 and *Antigone* 1308–9); the sharpened tongue: 584; the flesh cut by words: 786; the misfortune that pierces the liver: 938.

19. Jean Starobinski, "L'épée d'Ajax," in *Trois fureurs* (Paris: Gallimard, 1974), particularly pp. 27–29 and 61. See also D. Cohen, "The Imagery of Sophocles: A Study of Ajax' Suicide," *Greece and Rome,* 25 (1978), 24–36, and Charles Segal, "Visual Symbolism and Visual Effects in Sophocles," *Classical World,* 74 (1981), 125–142.

20. Haemon: *Antigone* 1175 (see also 1239). On *haima* as a word for effusion of blood, see H. Koller, "*Haima,*" *Glotta,* 15 (1967), 149–155.

21. *Schismos:* Aeschylus, *Agamemnon* 1149 (Cassandra); *schizō:* Sophocles, *Electra* 99 (murder of Agamemnon). *Daizō:* Aeschylus, *Agamemnon* 207–208 (sacrifice of Iphigenia), *Choephoroe* 860, 1071 (murder).

22. The blood law: Casabona, *Vocabulaire,* p. 160. Compare in Euripides' *Electra* the presence of sacrificial equipment (*kanoun, sphagis*) in the description of Clytemnestra's murder (1142; cf. 1222: *katarchomai,* commented on by P. Stengel, *Opferbraüche der Griechen,* Leipzig and Berlin: Teubner, 1910, p. 42). Eurydice is a *sphagion: Antigone* 1291, with the commentary of Casabona, *Vocabulaire,* p. 187. See also the remarks in the text commentary by R. C. Jebb (Cambridge: Cambridge University

Press, 1900) on *bōmia* (suicide at the foot of the altar) and the suicide's sword as sacrificial knife (1301).

23. See, for example, Euripides, *Helen* 353–359.

24. *Hippolytus* 1236–37, 1244–45. In his agony of pain, the dying Hippolytus, caught in a snare like Heracles, will ask for a flesh-cutting sword that will deliver him (1357; cf. Sophocles, *Trachiniae* 1031–33).

25. I deliberately use this phrase, which is logically impossible, for the text of the *Phoenissae* not only does not specify which of the two swords she uses, but even suggests in a general way that the common sword of the sons is involved (see 1456 and 1578).

26. R. Hirzel, "Der Selbstmord," *Archiv für Religionswissenschaft*, 11 (1908), especially pp. 256–258.

27. One can compare *Oedipus Tyrannus,* where Jocasta is *pantelēs damar* (accomplished wife), and the *Phoenissae,* where Jocasta dies "with" her sons and will be buried with them (1282, 1483, 1553–54, 1635). In the same way Eurydice is *pammētor,* entirely given to maternity (*Antigone* 1282).

28. "Le lit, la guerre," *L'Homme,* 21 (1981), 37–67. See also *"Ponos.* Sur quelques difficultés de la peine comme nom du travail," *Annali dell' Instituto Orientale di Napoli,* 4 (1982), 171–192.

29. Rope or sword: for Helen, if she had been a *gennaia gynē* (*Troades* 1012–14); for Creusa, if her death plan should fail (*Ion* 1063–65); for the manlike Electra (*Orestes,* 953), who would prefer the sword (1041, 1052); for the boastful Hermione (*Andromache* 811–813, 841–844), whose nurse dreads above all her hanging herself (815–816); for Admetus (*Alcestis* 227–229). See again *Andromache* 412, as well as *Hercules Furens* 319–320 and 1147–51.

30. I differ here from the interpretation of Casabona, *Vocabulaire,* p. 161. One should add that the verb *oregomai* used by the heroine is more suited to the act of wounding (frequent in the *Iliad*) than to that of knotting.

31. Hanging is mentioned by Orestes (Aeschylus, *Eumenides* 746; Euripides, *Orestes* 1062–63) and by Oedipus (Sophocles, *Oedipus Tyrannus* 1374; Euripides, *Phoenissae* 331–334.

32. See P. Chantraine, *Dictionnaire étymologique de la langue grecque,* s.v. *aeirō* (I, 23, on the derivative *aiōra*). Jocasta's *eōra:* Sophocles, *Oedipus Tyrannus* 1264. A controversy rages among historians of religion about the Athenian *aiōra,* the festival of suspension and balancing during which young girls play on swings while dolls hang in the branches of trees. Is it

a rural fertility rite? Or an expiatory rite? I do not intend to examine the difficult question here. See, for example, R. Martin and H. Metzger, *La religion grecque* (Paris: Presses Universitaires de France, 1976), pp. 127–128. I will simply recall that this feast finds its *aition* in the suicide of Erigone and the hanging of a young girl.

33. *Bathy ptōma:* Aeschylus, *Supplices* 796–797. *Aeirō:* for example, *Hippolytus* 735 (escape ode) and 779 (*ērtēmenē,* from *artaō,* derivative of *aeirō*), *Andromache* 848, 861–862. The depth of the ether: *Medea* 1295.

34. Wings, flight: *Medea* 1297, *Hercules Furens* 1158, *Hecuba* 1110, *Ion* 796–797 and 1239, *Helen* 1516. The bird: *Hippolytus* 733 (the chorus), 759, 828 (Phaedra); *Andromache* 861–862 (Hermione); *Iphigenia in Tauris* 1089, 1095–96 (*apteros ornis pothousa*); *Helen* 1478–94. On the bird caught in the snare and the hanged woman, see Loraux, "Le corps étranglé."

35. And, in another mode, womanly men, e.g., Jason; or Heracles, who, after committing feminine crime of murdering children, dreams of flying away (before giving up suicide and recovering his manhood); or Polymestor, mutilated by women and slaves. Flight: Aeschylus, *Supplices* 806; Euripides, *Ion* 1239.

36. Euripides, *Alcestis* 262–263 (image of the journey), 392, 394; *Suppliant Women* 1039, 1043, and 1017; *Hippolytus* 828–829.

37. Sophocles, *Ajax* 815 and 833. Lycophron (*Alexandra* 466) will also talk of *pēdēma.*

38. Aristotle, *Politics* I.13.1260a30, after Sophocles, *Ajax* 293 (it is the "eternal refrain" with which Ajax answers Tecmessa's questions); Euripides, *Heraclidae* 474–477.

39. Sophocles, *Trachiniae, Antigone, Oedipus Tyrannus* 1073–75 (with the remarks of Jebb on *siōpē* and its difference from *sigē*).

40. *Hippolytus* 828, *Trachiniae* 881 (*diēistōsen* is derived from *aistos,* invisible). Much could be made of the play between seeing and looking in the account of Deianira's death.

41. On the bolted interior and the opening of the doors, see *Oedipus Tyrannus* 1261–62 and *Hippolytus* 782, 793, 808, and 825 (note the use of the verb *chalan* in connection with the opening of the bolts, a verb that in *Oedipus Tyrannus* 1266 describes the unknotting of Jocasta's rope).

42. *Antigone* 1293 (and 1295, 1299). On *mychos,* the innermost cavity of the house, and the word's relation to femininity, see J.-P. Vernant, "Hestia-Hermes," in *Mythe et pensée chez les grecs,* I (Paris: François Maspéro, 1971), 152. In this connection one will note with Emily Vermeule (*Aspects of Death in Early Greek Art and Poetry,* Berkeley and London:

University of California Press, 1979, pp. 167–169) that the death of women, being always implicitly eroticized, is drawn to the hollow and the deep.

43. Note that Phaedra is no longer named. When they talk of her corpse, Theseus and Hippolytus talk of "that woman" (958) or use the word *sōma* (1009).

44. It is not certain that this was in fact the case, and a controversy rages on this death, as on many deaths in tragedy. See, for example, A. M. Dale, "Seen and Unseen on the Greek Stage," in *Collected Papers,* ed. T. B. L. Webster and E. G. Turner (Cambridge: Cambridge University Press, 1969), pp. 120–121; and C. P. Gardiner, "The Staging of the Death of Ajax," *Classical Journal,* 75 (1979), 10–14.

45. The body of the hero: *Ajax* 915–919, 992–993, 1001, 1003–4. The body of the warrior fallen in battle is, on the contrary, "noble": cf. J.-P. Vernant, "La belle mort et le cadavre outragé," in *La mort, les morts dans les sociétés anciennes,* ed. G. Gnoli and J.-P. Vernant (Cambridge and Paris: Cambridge University Press, 1982), pp. 45–76.

46. Alcestis dies onstage: 397–398. From 606 the funeral convoy is ready, but the intervention of the old father of Admetus leads to the setting up of a *prothesis* (between 608 and 740; see also 1012).

47. The most obvious case is that of Alcestis, who pursues conjugal devotion to the point of dying in her husband's place. Euripides' text uses many prepositions (*pro, hyper, peri* or *anti*) to express this exaggerated version of marital exchange: *Alcestis* 18, 37, 155, 178, 282–283, 284, 433–434, 460–463, 620, 682, 698, 1002. In this assemblage of women who die for men, Leda, who died for her daughter, is an exception, which one should perhaps link up with the theme of Demeter and Kore in the *Helen.*

48. Sophocles, *Trachiniae* 913; Euripides, *Alcestis* 175, 187, and 248–249; *Suppliant Women* 980 (see 1022: the *thalamos* of Persephone). *Thalamos* and marriage: see, for example, V. Magnien, "Le mariage chez les grecs anciens. L'initiation nuptiale," *L'Antiquité Classique,* 5 (1936), 115–117.

49. See Sophocles, *Trachiniae* 918–922, *Oedipus Tyrannus* 1242–43, 1249; also Euripides, *Alcestis* 175, 177, 183, 186–188, 249.

50. *Odyssey* XI.278: Epicaste attaches the rope *aph' hypsēloio melathrou;* Euripides, *Hippolytus* 769–770: *teramnon apo nymphidiōn. Melathron,* rooftree: R. Martin, "Le palais d'Ulysse et les inscriptions de Delos," in *Recueil Plassart* (Paris, 1976), pp. 126–129 (with references); *melathron* as metonymy of the palace: *Iliad* II.414, *Odyssey* XVII.150; *melathron* as metonymy of the nuptial abode: Euripides, *Iphigenia in*

Tauris 375–376. *Melathron* and the husband: Sappho, fr. III Campbell (with the translation of D. A. Campbell in *Greek Lyric,* Cambridge, Mass., and London: Harvard University Press, 1982).

51. Thus Admetus invites Alcestis to wait for him in Hades to "live with him there": Euripides, *Alcestis* 364. Furthermore, he at the same time expresses the normally feminine wish to lie at Alcestis' side (366, 897–902).

52. Aeschylus, *Choephoroe* 905–907, also 894–895 and 979 (Clytemnestra); *Agamemnon* 1441–47 (Cassandra, who indeed accepted this "dying with": *Agamemnon* 1139 and 1313–14).

53. I am alluding to the *Palinodia* by which the poet Stesichorus, after having like Homer "spoken ill" of Helen, substituted a phantom for the adulterous woman, which followed Paris to Troy. Meanwhile the real Helen, a model of virtue, spent the duration of the Trojan War in Egypt. Pledge to die: Euripides, *Helen* 837, a declaration echoed by Menelaus in 985–986.

54. Joint tomb: Euripides, *Suppliant Women* 1002–3; *synthanein:* 1007, 1040, 1063 (1071); union of bodies: 1019–21.

55. *Phoenissae* 1458–59 (*en toisi philtatois*); in 1578 she falls *amphi teknoisi* ("among" or "around") her sons.

56. I borrow this expression from an article by C. Nancy, "Euripide et le parti des femmes," in *La femme dans les sociétés antiques,* ed. E. Lévy (Strasbourg: Université des Sciences Humaines de Strasbourg, 1983).

57. The best (*aristē, esthlē, philtatē*) of women: Euripides, *Alcestis* 83–85, 151–152, 200, 231, 235–236, 241–242, etc.; the last word: 391; death accepted: 17 (*thelein,* verb of the hoplite imperative; cf. 155); glorious death: 150 (see 157 and 453–454); boldness: 462, 623–624 and 741; nobility: 742, 994.

58. Virility, glory, and boldness: Euripides, *Suppliant Women* 987, 1013, 1014–16, 1055 (*kleinon*), 1059, 1067; the nuptial/funeral adornment of Evadne: 1055; beyond femininity: 1062–63; this side of virility: 1075. Other examples of feminine glory in Euripides: *Helen* 302, *Hecuba* 1282–83.

59. I have expanded on this in "La gloire et la mort d'une femme," *Sorcières,* 18 (1979), 51–57.

II. The Pure Blood of Virgins

1. *Antigone* 773, 780. On the similarities and differences between the killing of Antigone and that of the Vestal *incesta,* I refer to a study by Augusto Fraschetti, not yet published.

2. For *sphazō*, see chap. I, note 22. *Thyō* and its derivatives: Aeschylus, *Agamemnon* 214–215, 224–225, 235–241, 1417; Sophocles, *Electra* 531–532, 572–573. *Phonos* and *phoneuō*: *Iphigenia in Aulis* 512, 939, and, above all, 1317–18; Clytemnestra in this play always describes the sacrifice of Iphigenia as an execution (*ktanō*). Note that in Aeschylus criticism is heard from every side, despite the use of the verb *thyō*—but the sacrifice will rebound against Agamemnon, "sacrificed" by Clytemnestra (*Agamemnon* 1503).

3. See the work of J.-L. Durand on the Bouphonia (especially "Le corps du délit," *Communications,* 26 [1977], 46–61); also, on the staging of sacrifice, the remarks of J.-P. Vernant, "Sacrifice et mise à mort dans la *thusia* grecque," in *Le sacrifice dans l'antiquité,* Entretiens de la Fondations Hardt, vol. 27 (Vandoeuvres-Geneva, 1981), 1–18 and 22.

4. Sacrifice was not *shown* to the spectators, but from the point of view of the *logos* it was submitted to no censure, and the messengers gave long and detailed accounts. One finds, at the level of discourse, what J.-L. Durand remarked about figurative representations, that "human sacrifice is pleasurable to contemplate if projected in imagination" ("Bêtes grecques," in *La cuisine du sacrifice,* p. 138). On human sacrifice as fiction, see also the remarks of A. Henrichs, "Human Sacrifice in Greek Religion: Three Case Studies," in *Le sacrifice dans l'antiquité,* pp. 195–235.

5. *Parthenos* and war: J.-P. Vernant, "City-State Warfare," in *Myth and Society in Ancient Greece* (Brighton: Harvester Press, 1980), p. 24. Shedding the blood of one girl to save the community of *andres:* the reasoning is explicit in the fragment of Euripides' *Erechtheus,* quoted by Lycurgus (*Against Leocrates* 100.22–39); see Loraux, "Le lit, la guerre," pp. 42–43.

6. Euripides, *Hecuba* 525–527, 544: *lektoi t' Achaiōn ekkritoi neaniai, logades.* All the *parthenoi* sacrificed were not called Polycrites ("the much-chosen": cf. W. Burkert, *Structure and History in Greek Mythology and Ritual,* Los Angeles and London: University of California Press, 1979, p. 73), but all were "chosen."

7. Euripides, *Hecuba* 537 (*akraiphnes haim'*), *Iphigenia in Aulis* 1574 (*achranton haima*). Although purity of blood is metonymic with purity of the virgin, Pausanias' account about the daughter of Aristodamus dispenses with this metonymy, and it is the virgin due for sacrifice who is called *achrantos,* pure (IV.9.4). *Chrainō:* touch, hence defile . . .

8. Aeschylus, *Agamemnon* 232 and 1414–16 (which in the logic of the *Oresteia* one should compare with the *Eumenides* 450: the cycle of

defilement is closed, since the blood from the severed throat of a young animal [*boton*] has been poured on Orestes).

9. Euripides, *Iphigenia in Tauris* 359, *Iphigenia in Aulis* 1080–83.

10. On the sacrifice by Hermes in the *Homeric Hymn* dedicated to that god, see L. Kahn, *Hermès passe* (Paris: François Maspéro, 1978), especially pp. 41–73.

11. Quoted from P. Vidal-Naquet, "Hunting and Sacrifice in Aeschylus' *Oresteia*," in *Tragedy and Myth in Ancient Greece*, pp. 150–165 (p. 153). A doe substituted for a young girl (*Iphigenia in Aulis* 1587–89 and 1593): the oldest version of the story (A. Henrichs, "Human Sacrifice," p. 199), going back to the *Cypria*, opposed by a more widespread version (Aeschylus, Pindar, Sophocles) in which the virgin was actually sacrificed. See F. Jouan, *Euripide et les légendes des Chants Cypriens* (Paris: Les Belles Lettres, 1966), pp. 273–274.

12. Euripides, *Hecuba* 205–206 (comparison), 526 (metaphor; in the *Alexandra* of Lycophron, 327, Polyxena is *stephēphoros bous*, a heifer adorned with strips of cloth); 142: *pōlos*.

13. As Stella Georgoudi has pointed out to me, *pōlodamnein* describes the act of training a colt to make it a horse. There is no such verb in Greek as *hippodamnein*.

14. See V. Magnien, "Vocabulaire grec reflétant les rites du mariage," in *Mélanges Desrousseaux* (Paris: Hachette, 1937), pp. 293–297, and "Le mariage chez les grecs anciens," *L'Antiquité Classique*, 5 (1936), especially pp. 129–131; also C. Calame, *Les choeurs de jeunes filles dans la Grèce archaïque*, I (Rome: Edizioni dell' Atenco e Bizzarri, 1977), 411–420, and M. Detienne, "Puissances du mariage," in *Dictionnaire des mythologies*, ed. Y. Bonnefoy, II (Paris: Flammarion, 1981), 67.

15. In *Iphigenia in Aulis* 1113, Agamemnon plays on a double meaning when he announces that the *moschoi* are ready for the prenuptial sacrifice of the *proteleia*.

16. The story of the daughter of Aristodamus (Pausanias IV.9.4–10) is enlightening. When he disputes that Aristodamus is still *kyrios* over his daughter, the betrothed of the young girl reminds him that, in the intermediate stage in which the *nymphē* finds herself, the passage from one *kyrios* to another is already complete. Aristodamus has "given" his daughter in marriage, so he cannot "give" her to be sacrificed. See on this subject P. Roussel, "Le role d'Achille dans *l'Iphigénie à Aulis*," *Revue des Etudes Grecques*, 28 (1915), especially p. 249, and "Le thème du sacrifice volontaire dans la tragédie d'Euripide," *Revue Belge de Philologie et d'Histoire*, 1 (1922), especially pp. 234–235; also the observations of J. Red-

field, "Notes on the Greek Wedding," *Arethusa,* 15 (1982), 181–201 (p. 187).

17. If, in the middle voice, *agomai* means (for the man) "to take" a wife and marry her, the passive form *agomai* is appropriate to the young girl in that it means "to be led away," referring to the victim (*agō* in sacrificial language: Porphyry, *De abstinentia* II.28.1). Ambiguity in tragedy of the verb *agein: Iphigenia in Aulis* 434, 714 (and passim, so much is it the principal characteristic of Iphigenia to be "led"); *Hecuba* 43–44, 222–223, 369, 432 (Polyxena). See also Sophocles, *Antigone* 773, 885 (and 811, 916) and the "leading" of Alcestis by Thanatos (Euripides, *Alcestis* 259).

18. In the *Agamemnon,* the father is the sacrificer (209–211, 224–225) even though at the supreme moment the sacrificers are increased in number (240–241). In *Iphigenia in Aulis* he is relieved at the last moment by Calchas: see Jouan, *Euripide,* pp. 277 and 288, and note in *Iphigenia in Aulis* (Belles Lettres, Paris: Collections des Universités de France, 1983), pp. 26–27 (with bibliographical references on the debate about the authenticity of this passage). On the literary theme of the sacrificing father, see E. Pellizer, *Favole d'identità, favole di paura* (Rome: Istituto della Enciclopedia Italiana, 1982), pp. 102–103.

19. *Hecuba* 523 (same gesture on the hydria of Berlin 1902). One will remember with C. Leduc that *engyē* was originally a palmful or "pledge in the hand" ("Réflexions sur le système matrimonial athénien à l'époque de la cité-état," in *La Dot. La valeur des femmes,* Toulouse: Université de Toulouse-Le Mirail, 1982, p. 13).

20. On this question see W. Burkert, *Homo necans: The Anthropology of Ancient Greek Sacrificial Ritual and Myth* (Berkeley, Los Angeles, and London: University of California Press, 1983), pp. 58–67, as well as the discussion between J. Rudhardt, A. Henrichs, G. Piccaluga, and W. Burkert in *Le sacrifice dans l'antiquité,* pp. 236–238.

21. See L. Kahn and N. Loraux, "Mythes de la mort," in *Dictionnaire des mythologies,* II, 121–124. Similarities between the marriage and the funeral ceremonies: Redfield, "Notes," pp. 188–191.

22. It is, as far as I can see, tragedy that brings about this reversal. The theme of marriage in Hades will be taken up in epitaphs from the Hellenistic period onward, and in many epigrams in the *Palatine Anthology,* but if we exclude the famous and difficult epitaph of Phrasikleia (Peek, *Griechische Vers-Inschriften,* no. 68), the funerary poetry of the archaic and classical periods does not associate this theme with the death of young girls.

23. As they refuse marriage, the Danaids prefer the rope to male contact and the dominance of Hades to that of a husband (Aeschylus, *Supplices* 787–791). However, while the Danaids pretend not to know it, the spectator for his part knows that, in exchanging one master for another, they will simply substitute a "husband" for a husband.

24. Marriage in Hades: *Antigone* 653–654; marriage with Acheron: 810–816; *lithostrōton korēs nympheion Haidou:* 1204–5; see also 568, 575, 796–797, 804 (*thalamos*), 891–892 (*tymbos, nympheion*). On Antigone-Kore, see the remarks of C. P. Segal, *Tragedy and Civilization* (Cambridge, Mass., and London: Harvard University Press, 1981), pp. 152–206.

25. Euripides, *Iphigenia in Tauris* 369. See also *Iphigenia in Aulis* 461, 540, 1278; the linking of marriage with sacrifice, already noticeable in *Iphigenia in Tauris* (216, 364–371: *haimatērōn gamōn,* 818–819, 856–861), dominates *Iphigenia in Aulis* throughout. See, for example, H. P. Foley, "Marriage and Sacrifice in Euripides' *Iphigenia in Aulis,*" *Arethusa,* 15 (1982), 159–180.

26. From Lycophron (*Alexandra* 323) to Seneca and beyond, the theme of Polyxena's death as "nuptial sacrifice" is Hellenistic and Roman (A. Fontinoy, "Le sacrifice nuptial de Polyxène," *L'Antiquité Classique,* 19 [1950], 383–396).

27. Euripides, *Hecuba* 352–353 (*nymphē*), 368 (*Hades*), 414–416, and, above all, 611–612.

28. L. Méridier, commenting on line 612 (Belles Lettres edition).

29. Macaria sacrificed to Kore: Euripides, *Heraclidae* 409–410, 490, 601; Hades: 514; the moment of marriage against her brothers' lives: 579–580; death for her *genos:* 590; children and *partheneia:* 591–592.

30. L. Méridier, commenting on line 592 (Belles Lettres). See also the translation by P. Vellacott, *Ironic Drama* (Cambridge, Mass., and London: Harvard University Press, 1975), p. 191 ("for babes unborn, maidenhead unfulfilled"). One would prefer Marie Delcourt's translation (Gallimard, "La Pléiade"): "trésor qui me tient lieu d'enfants, de ma virginité offerte."

31. This theme appears even in the case of male infants: Euripides, *Hercules Furens* 481–484 (Megara offering her sons the Keres as wives), *Troades* 1218–20 (funerary/nuptial adornment of Astyanax).

32. This supposes a certain treatment of the female body, in which the throat is imbued with sexual values. I shall return to this, p. 61.

33. One *gēgenes* for another. In autochthonous language this is expressed *anti karpou karpon* (a fruit in place of a fruit: Euripides, *Phoenissae* 931–941). Note that, being Spartos by his father and mother (994–996),

Menoeceus is, as it were, born of the fatherland (996). In Spartan language there is no mother other than the land of their fathers (again mentioned 913, 918, 947–948, 969, 1056).

34. *Phoenissae* 1009 (standing up, *stas,* like a hoplite)–1012 ("I will free my land"), and 1090–92.

35. *Phoenissae* 942–948, commented on by Roussel, "Le rôle d'Achille," p. 243.

36. To qualify J.-P. Vernant's phrase, which maintains that "marriage to a girl is what war is to a boy" ("La guerre des cités," p. 38), see the remarks of P. Schmitt-Pantel, "Histoire de tyran," in *Les marginaux et les exclus dans l'histoire,* ed. B. Vincent (Paris: Union Générale d'Editions, 1979), pp. 217–231, especially 226–227.

37. If we are to believe Plutarch (*Quaestiones conviviales* VIII.8.3), a special order from Delphi was required for men to start sacrificing animals, "and now one never cuts the throat of an animal before it has bowed its head under a libation of pure water and has by this sign consented to the fate planned for it." See, for example, Roussel, "Le thème du sacrifice volontaire," and W. Burkert, "Greek Tragedy and Sacrificial Ritual," *Greek, Roman and Byzantine Studies,* 7 (1966), especially pp. 106–107.

38. This choice reinforces the decision to make Iphigenia actually die. Cf. A. Henrichs, "Human Sacrifice," p. 199.

39. Whereas a silence of good omen should accompany a sacrifice, and in contrast *euphēmia* surrounds the sacrifice in *Iphigenia in Aulis:* 1467–69, 1560, 1564 (see also *Hecuba* 530 and 532–533: the sacrifice of Polyxena).

40. Defilement, impurity, impiety: Aeschylus, *Agamemnon* 209, 220; virginal age: 228–230; violence: 232–240.

41. Another young girl in Aeschylus, Cassandra, refuses to regard her murder as a sacrifice. She knows that the block awaits her in the guise of an altar (*Agamemnon* 1277). She wants to be courageous (1290) but refuses to let the chorus regularize her situation by comparing her to a heifer, impelled by the gods as she marches bravely to the altar (1297–98 and 1299–1303).

42. *Agamemnon* 232–235. On Iphigenia looking for a refuge in the ground, see the remarks of J. Bollack, *L'Agamemnon d'Eschyle* (Lille and Paris: Presses Universitaires de Lille, 1981), I/2, pp. 295–298. It is not necessary to suppose, like Jouan (*Euripide,* p. 271, n. 5), that Aeschylus was here following the representation of Polyxena's sacrifice on a Tyrrhenian amphora in London. It is in fact probable that the painter and the poet,

each in his own language, followed sacrificial practice for a human victim, which consisted in "hoisting" (*aeirō, airesthai*) the victim. See Stengel, *Opferbraüche*, pp. 105–112, and Casabona, *Vocabulaire*, p. 162. *Aerdēn* (or *ardēn*) is an adverb derived from *aeirō*. If one agrees with Redfield ("Notes," pp. 191–192 and 198, n. 5) that hoisting the bride off the ground at the wedding amounted to dramatizing her inevitable refusal to acquiesce, one might perhaps uncover in Aeschylus' text yet another link between sacrifice and marriage. In any case, as the violence is in no way feigned, only the sacrificial interpretation seems to be relevant here.

43. *Iphigenia in Tauris* 26–27. Here is a word-for-word "quotation" from Aeschylus (*metarsia,* an adjective derived from *aeirō,* harking back to *aerdēn*). On this problem, see R. Aelion, *Euripide héritier d'Eschyle* (Paris: Les Belles Lettres, 1983) I, 106–107 and II, 117.

44. *Iphigenia in Aulis* 1587 and 1589 (*ardēn*). Jouan's translation ("son sang ruisselait à flots sur l'autel de la déesse") does not give the word *ardēn* its topical meaning.

45. *Hecuba* 525–527. The "chosen" Achaeans (the élite of the young warriors) have "to hold back with their arms the leaps [*skirtēma*] of the young heifer" Polyxena. In fact *skirtaō* is used of young animals, *pōloi* or goats (Theocritus I.152).

46. *Hecuba* 545, 548–550, 554, 561. A passage in the *Ajax* clearly indicates that in kneeling down, whether one is a suppliant or not, the essential thing is to cling to the ground (1180–81).

47. On the contrary, in a depiction inside a vase, the bent knee of Cassandra is imploring as Clytemnestra raises her ax on her (cf. N. Alfieri, P. E. Arias, and M. Hirmer, *Spina,* Munich: Hirmer Verlag, 1958, p. 59 and pl. 99: ca. 430 B.C.). Was this a barbarian gesture? Or a gesture of distress? Or both at the same time, as in Aeschylus, *Persae* 929–930?

48. See *Planudean Anthology* IV.150 (description of a Polyxena on her knees "begging for her life"). Similarly, in Lucretius there is a suppliant Iphigenia (Iphianassa) who bends her knee before being "hoisted up by men's hands and led to the altar" (*De rerum natura* I.92 and 95).

49. Besides the Tyrrhenian amphora in London (97-7-272), one should mention the one in Berlin (4841).

50. In the description of Polyxena, Euripides reverses some of the traits of Aeschylus' Iphigenia (cf. J. Schmitt, *Freiwilligen Opfertod bei Euripides,* Giessen, 1921, pp. 57–58).

51. Macaria's freedom (501–502, 528–529, 550, 559) comes through her refusal to put her decision at the mercy of drawing lots. Refusal to die at the hands of males: 560–561, 565–566. On 821–822 and the reasons for

the silence observed on the killing (voluntary censorship or later reworking), I shall not express a view.

52. The difference can be measured by making a comparison with the story of Aristodamus' daughter (Pausanias IV.9.4 and 6), in which it is the father who must give his daughter away with his full approval (*hekousios, hekōn*). In *Iphigenia in Aulis,* it is Agamemnon who acts in spite of himself, *akōn* (1157).

53. For example, Katsouris, "Suicide Motive," n. 9 and pp. 16 and 21.

54. On the noble death, as opposed to suicide, see Loraux, *The Invention of Athens,* pp. 99–100, and "La belle mort spartiate," p. 108.

55. Erechtheus, fr. 65 Austin, 67, which can be compared with Herodotus I.30 (Tellus of Athens).

56. Erechtheus, fr. 65 Austin, 68–70. The common tomb and shared glory were the special reward of the *andres* for Praxithea: Lycurgus, *Against Leocrates* 100.32–33. Tragic irony . . .

57. See Nancy, "Euripide et le parti des femmes," pp. 85–88, and Vellacott, *Ironic Drama,* pp. 178–204.

58. Menoeceus dies standing up (*Phoenissae* 1009, 1091), like a warrior (1001–2). He wins the admiration of the chorus for his victory (1054–57: *kallinika;* cf. 1314: *onoma gennaion*). In the *Troades,* Cassandra anticipates his victorious arrival (*nikēphoros:* 460) among the dead. On the *tolma* and *eukleia* of Cassandra, see also Aeschylus, *Agamemnon* 1302, 1304.

59. Sophocles, *Antigone* 817–822 (*autonomos;* see also 502–504, 694–695); but this glory is ambiguous, as the young girl guesses: 836–839 and 853.

60. Macaria: *Heraclidae,* especially 533–534, 627–628 (the death of the *agathoi,* topical description of martial death). Polyxena: *Hecuba,* especially 348, 380–381, and 592 (nobility). Iphigenia: compare *Iphigenia in Aulis* 1252 (refusal of the noble death) and 1374–75 (*eukleōs*), 1398 (memory), 1423–24 (nobility), 1504 (immortal glory). The paean of Artemis is sung by the chorus for Iphigenia, and by women for a virgin (and yet the paean is usually masculine: Calame, *Les choeurs de jeunes filles,* I, 148–149).

61. On this subject see the remarks of G. B. Walsh, *Classical Philology,* 69 (1974), 241–248. *Aretē* for Iphigenia and, consequently, *aidōs,* a feminine virtue, for Achilles.

62. During a reading of this text, Ileana Chirassi-Colombo drew my attention to a passage of the *Metamorphoses* (XIII.692–699) in which Ovid draws a most radical consequence from this law, changing the bod-

ies of Orion's daughters, who killed themselves for their country, into *juvenes*. But the metamorphosis is foreign to the logic of tragedy, which prefers to stick to the resources of discourse.

63. If tragedy is feminist, it is so in the style of those feminists mentioned by P. Darmon, who "revive the feminine gender in a bath of blood" (*Mythologie de la femme dans l'ancienne France*, Paris: Le Seuil, 1983, p. 59).

III. Regions of the Body

1. For example, consider Mazon's translation (Belles Lettres) of 271–272 of the *Choephoroe*, where "the warm liver" becomes "the blood of my heart," for reasons that Mazon details clearly in a note where the issue is well laid out—between transposition and a "literal" translation, which latter can be indicated only at the foot of the page. On these questions, see also the remarks of Mazon's disciple, J. Dumortier, in the introduction to his work, *Le vocabulaire médical d'Eschyle et les écrits hippocratiques* (Paris: Les Belles Lettres, 1935).

2. For example, *Helen* 354 and *Hippolytus* 781.

3. See Chantraine, *Dictionnaire étymologique*, s.v. *auchēn* and *derē*. Throat of Aphrodite; *Iliad* III.39 (and *Homeric Hymn to Aphrodite* 88); throat of the loved girl: Sappho, fr. 216 Page, 16; neck of Medea: Euripides, *Medea* 30–31; mourning: Euripides, *Electra* 146–147.

4. On *sphazō* as the word for throat-cutting, on the equivalence of *sphazō* and *deirotomeō* (slice the throat), and on *sphagē* as a word for the throat, see Casabona, *Vocabulaire*, pp. 155–156 and 175.

5. *Iphigenia in Tauris* 853–854 (cf. 1460); *Iphigenia in Aulis* 1430 (and 1516, 1560, 1574); *Hecuba* 151–153. Of course, the immolation of a man, if it took place, would also be carried out at the throat; *Hercules Furens* 319–320 (but it so happens that this type of immolation never in fact took place).

6. *Derē* and the knife on the throat: for example, *Orestes* 1194, 1349, 1575; *laimos* and the act of sacrifice: *Heraclidae* 822, *Phoenissae* 1421, *Iphigenia in Aulis* 1579. *Laimos* is also Polyxena's throat when she is considered as a sacrificial victim (*Hecuba* 565; in 567, Neoptolemus cuts the "breath passage"). *Laimotomos* (*laimotmētos*) characterizes the Gorgon, with her throat cut: *Ion* 1054, *Electra* 549, *Phoenissae* 455.

7. Euripides, *Orestes* 1471–73, with the note of Chapouthier (Belles Lettres) and that of Delcourt (Gallimard, "La Pléiade"). On the

significance of the gesture that bends the victim's neck upward or downward, see Stengel, *Opferbraüche,* pp. 113–125.

8. Euripides, *Electra* 1223, also 485 (in 1222 Orestes uses the "sacrificial" verb *katarkhomai,* and in 1228 Clytemnestra's wound is described as *sphagas*). Already in Aeschylus Clytemnestra was struck in the throat: *Eumenides* 592 (*pros derēn temōn*), also *Choephoroe* 883–884 (*auchēn*).

9. See *Helen* 355–356 (in Helen's plans for suicide, *laimotomon sphagas* is the alternative to hanging).

10. Even Aegisthus, whose death in Euripides is involved in the sacrifice on which he had embarked, was not struck in the throat, but in the vertebrae, by Orestes, who smashed his back (*Electra* 841–842).

11. *Tropōn tōn autōn: Choephoroe* 274; the ax blow full on the brow: Sophocles, *Electra* 95–99 and 195.

12. The neck, weak point: *Iliad* XXII.321–327 (death of Hector), also VIII.325–326 and XXIII.821; warriors with their throats sliced: XIII.202, XVII.49, XXI.555 (*deirotomeō*). See also Hesiod, *The Shield* 418 (Cycnus killed in the neck). In Homer, C. Daremberg (*La médecine dans Homère,* Paris: Didier, 1865, pp. 14–15 and 38) counts six wounds in the throat and sixty-two in the neck. The purely functional reasons advanced by M. D. Grmek (*Les maladies à l'aube de la civilisation occidentale,* Paris: Payot, 1983, p. 55) are probably inadequate to explain the recurrence of such a wound in the epic.

13. *Phoenissae* 1288–92; civil war (*stasis*) and *sphagē:* see M. Detienne and J. Svenbro, "Les loups au festin ou la cité impossible," in *La cuisine du sacrifice,* p. 231.

14. Euripides, *Medea* 30, *Iphigenia in Aulis* 875. One can appreciate the difference from the *Iliad,* where the neck, seen as white and tender at the moment the steel cuts, is the man's neck, because only the warrior's body is eroticized. See Vermeule, *Aspects of Death,* pp. 101–105.

15. All these places of death are taken from one book, i.e., IV.457–531. On the essential vulnerability of the man's body in Homer, see Vermeule, *Aspects of Death,* pp. 96–97.

16. The protected side: Euripides, *Troades* 1137, *Heraclidae* 824; the wounded side: Aeschylus, *Seven against Thebes* 624 and especially 888–890 (description by the chorus of the death of the sons of Oedipus by the left side—the unusual, sinister side—*di' eyōnymōn tetymmenoi . . . homosplanchnōn te pleurōmatōn,* a passage parodied by Euripides in *Phoenissae* 1288–92).

17. Euripides, *Andromache* 1150; in 1120, Neoptolemus has not been "hit in the right spot," and in 1132–34 he has been riddled with projectiles of various kinds (stones, darts, arrows, etc.).

18. Wounded through the navel (*Phoenissae* 1412–13), Polynices falls, bending *pleura kai nēdyn*. The image of the sword through the lungs/through the side: compare Aeschylus, *Choephoroe* 639–640; Euripides, *Ion* 765–767; and Aeschylus, *Eumenides* 843.

19. *Erechtheus,* fr. 65 Austin, 15; *Phoenissae* 1421 and 1437–41; *Medea,* 379.

20. Haemon: *Antigone* 1236 (*pleurais*); Ajax: Sophocles, *Ajax* 834 (*pleuran*) (cf. Pindar, *Nemean* VII.25: *dia phrenōn;* on the wound in the diaphragm, see Dumortier, *Le vocabulaire médical d'Eschyle,* p. 11).

21. Euripides, *Hercules Furens* 1149, *Helen* 982–983, *Orestes* 1062–63 (*eugeneia*). Note that one of the themes of the *Orestes* is the contrast between *sphagē,* a method of murder, and a voluntary, noble death, which is administered by a blow in the liver.

22. Aeschylus, *Agamemnon* 432, 792, *Choephoroe* 272, *Eumenides* 135 (and 158); Sophocles, *Ajax* 938; Euripides, *Suppliant Women* 599, *Hippolytus* 1070.

23. Sophocles, *Antigone* 1315–16 (*hyph' hēpar*), 1291–92 (*sphagiōn*), 1301 (*bōmia*), 1283 (*plēgmasin*), 1314 (*en phonais;* cf. 696, where the warrior death of Polynices occurred *en phonais*).

24. The nurse has been "companion in the ranks" (*parastasis: Trachiniae* 889) of Deianira's suicide, which was still solitary. It is worth recalling that the notion of *parastasis* forms the basis of a phalanx's order of hoplites.

25. Which must be interpreted in the logic of the text, and not, as G. Devereux has done in a study that is otherwise most attentive to word-for-word meaning in tragedy (*Tragédie et poésie grecques,* Paris: Flammarion, 1975, pp. 117–136), in the logic of someone's unconscious—that of Deianira or Sophocles (in whom this "masculinization" of the mild and tender wife could be put down to the "backlash of repressed feeling").

26. *Trachiniae* 923–926. Even though the brooch unfastened by Deianira may have held her dress between her two breasts, it is not her bosom that Heracles' wife exposes, but her arm and side.

27. The interpretation that attributes the passage as a whole to a slip of the pen (i.e., the view of Devereux, *Tragédie et poésie grecques,* pp. 114, 122, 136) is hardly more satisfying. What is more, to assign this "confusion" of right and left to Sophocles' "strong homosexual tendencies"

because "two categories, homosexuals and those who are lefthanded, tend to confuse left and right" (p. 137) is not a suggestion to be taken seriously. When one is reading a tragic text, it is important to remember that one is reading a text, and a very finely wrought one at that.

28. For the close correlation of right side/masculine and left side/feminine, see Nicole Loraux, "Héraklès, le surmâle et le féminin," *Revue Française de Psychanalyse,* 46 (1982), 725.

29. Note that in the *Trachiniae,* the connotations of the side can be erotic as well as warlike: see 930–939 and 1225–26 (cf. Euripides, *Hecuba* 826).

30. *Hecuba* 566–567. It is also in the throat that, in the *Alexandra* of Lycophron, the son of Achilles strikes Polyxena (326: *laimisas*).

31. It is in an entirely different context that Aristodamus, who killed his daughter to prove that she was not pregnant, sees her in a dream "with her breast and belly open" (Pausanias IV.13.2). As far as I know, no woman is killed through the breast in tragedy. As we have seen, Clytemnestra, in spite of using her *mastos* in a suppliant role, was struck in the throat; and it was the scene in the *Choephoroe* that influenced Mazon in his translation of *Eumenides* 84, when he wrote "piercing a mother's breast" where the text speaks only of "piercing the maternal body" (*mētrōion demas*).

32. Aristotle, *History of Animals* I.14.493b7 (*koinon meros auchenos kai stēthous sphagē*), commented on by Casabona, *Vocabulaire,* p. 175, n. 31.

33. The most common interpretation of *Agamemnon* 239 is that "the saffron dress" of Iphigenia "flows to the ground"; but there are good reasons for accepting another meaning, by which it is "the saffron hue" of the virgin's blood that is poured on the ground (see the demonstration of Bollack, *L'Agamemnon d'Eschyle,* I/2, pp. 300–303). If, as some commentators have thought, the sacrifice of Polyxena is a Euripidean reinterpretation of Aeschylus' lines, we would have to date from Euripides the traditional reading of this passage.

34. In the *Heraclidae,* Macaria alludes to an unveiling (561). J. Heckenbach (*De nuditate sacra sacrisque vinculis,* Giessen, 1911, pp. 9–10) queries this behavior as regards Polyxena. One might point out that this unveiling is like a brutal parody of the *anakalypsis* of the bride on marriage, which Seneca seems to imply, *Troades* 87–93.

35. Greek painting: see *Planudean Anthology* IV.150; Pietro da Cortona: I am thinking of the *Sacrifice of Polyxena* in the Capitol museum in Rome.

36. There are in Euripides twenty-seven occurrences of *mastos* as the

word for the maternal breast, against two uses in the erotic sense: *Andromache* 629 (see Aristophanes, *Lysistrata* 155–156) and *Cyclops* 170. I borrow the term "partial object" from the language of psychoanalysis: see J. Laplanche and J.-B. Pontalis, *Vocabulaire de la psychanalyse* (Paris: Presses Universitaires de France, 1967), pp. 294–295.

37. Euripides, *Suppliant Women* 604, *Phoenissae* 134, 162, 1375, 1397, 1437. Since Homer (*Iliad* XIII.288–290, XXII.282–285), the valiant warrior had to be hit in front, in the chest, and not in the back.

38. Electra: Euripides, *Orestes* 1049, *Electra* 1321; Iphigenia: *Iphigenia in Aulis* 634; the virginal beauty of Iphigenia: 681. Note that (1) the signs of beauty—the bosom, cheeks, and hair—are precisely what are spoiled in mourning, and (2) in Euripides' *Electra* (1023) it is by evoking the "white cheek" of Iphigenia that Clytemnestra sums up the scandal of the sacrifice. Mourning: *Suppliant Women* 87, 979, *Troades* 794, *Andromache* 832–834. The bosom "as of a statue" (*hōs agalmatos*), the source of Polyxena's beauty, evokes in a quite different key the Iphigenia of Aeschylus, jewel of her father's house (*Agamemnon* 208).

39. Note that the very rare association of *mastoi* and *sternon* appears once again in *Hecuba* (424: Polyxena's farewell to the softness of a mother's body).

40. *Hecuba* 208–210 (*nekrōn meta*); 568–570 (modesty).

41. Seneca, *Troades* 195–196, 202, 361–364, 940–944, and 1132 (the account of the sacrifice starts with *thalami more*).

42. Fontinoy ("Le sacrifice nuptial," p. 386) is surprised that the theme of marriage, essential in his view, is so little developed in the account of the sacrifice.

43. Ovid, *Metamorphoses* XIII.451–452, 458–459, 479–480. Euripides as model of Ovid and Seneca: Aelion, *Euripide héritier d'Eschyle*, II, 114, n. 9.

44. In the same book of the *Metamorphoses*, one of the daughters of Orion kills herself "with a courage exceeding her sex, by striking her naked breast" (XIII.693).

45. See G. Arrigoni, *Camilla, Amazzone e sacerdotessa di Diana* (Milan: Cisalpino-Goliardica, 1982), especially pp. 37–38 (right breast of Camilla). Note that Dido likewise strikes herself on the breast (*Aeneid* IV.689). The prose of the historians does not lag behind—Lucretia sinks the blade into her breast (Livy I.48.11), while Virginius strikes his daughter there to save her virginity (Livy III.48.5). Furthermore, it should be pointed out with Devereux (*Tragédie et poésie grecques*, p. 123) that in the Latin texts women generally kill themselves with a sword.

46. The other alternative starts with the words *hyp' auchena* (*Hecuba* 564). For Polyxena the nape is also the classic place for the yoke (*Hecuba* 376).

47. The death of the Amazon Penthesilea was already in archaic, and then in classical times, a *topos* for artistic representation. See, for example, Vermeule, *Aspects of Death*, p. 158; also D. von Bothmer, *Amazons in Greek Art* (London: Clarendon Press, 1957), IV, 2 and pl. LI (Attic black-figure amphora, London B 10).

48. I refer here to the analyses by Giulia Sissa of the women's bodies caught between the upper and lower mouth (*Le corps virginal*, Paris: Vrin, 1986). The cervix can be called *auchēn*, like the neck: see Hippocrates, *Diseases of Women* III.230 (also II.169: *trachēlos*, another name for the neck).

49. Hippocrates, *Diseases of Women* II.127, 151 (as well as 110, 126, 201, 203); on the place of this "hysterical aphonia" within the Hippocratic system of the "silences of the body," see M. G. Ciani, *Le regioni del silenzio* (Padua: Bloom Edizioni, 1983), pp. 157–172.

50. In this connection the Hippocratic treatise *Diseases of Young Girls* is remarkable. I analyze its essential ideas in "Le corps étranglé," p. 216.

51. S. Freud, *Standard Edition*, 24 vols. (London: Hogarth Press, 1953–1974), VII, 3–12.

52. Which, as Monique Schneider pointed out to me, has not always been prepared to bother about women's throats.

53. The figure of Medea is important in this respect, in that she refuses to turn death on herself. Killing, instead of killing herself, she sets a different logic in motion. Faced with it, the spectator no doubt finds it harder to profit from the imagination.

54. I borrow the expression "interference" from P. Vidal-Naquet in *Tragedy and Myth in Ancient Greece*.

55. At least this is so in those plays that, as a result of the Alexandrians' choice, have come down to us in their entirety. These make up the corpus which is available to everyone, and on which we have elected to work. To mention only Euripides, we should remember that, like Phaedra, his Laodamia and his Stheneboea committed suicide in tragedies that have been lost.

56. The famous *Katharsis* (Aristotle, *Poetics* 49b28), according to the translation by R. Dupont-Roc and J. Lallot (Paris, 1980); see their commentary on this passage, pp. 186–193.

CAST OF CHARACTERS

Achilles
: Very little present in tragedy, the hero of the *Iliad* was supposed at Aulis to be betrothed to Iphigenia. At Troy Polyxena was sacrificed on his tomb. See Euripides, *Hecuba, Iphigenia in Aulis.*

Admetus
: Husband of Alcestis. See Euripides, *Alcestis.*

Aegisthus
: Lover of Clytemnestra and cousin of Agamemnon. He helped her to kill the latter before being himself killed by Orestes. See Aeschylus, *Agamemnon, Choephoroe;* Euripides, *Electra.*

Agamemnon
: King of Argos and leader of the Greek expedition against Troy. Sacrificed his daughter Iphigenia and was eventually killed by his wife, Clytemnestra. See Aeschylus, *Agamemnon* and *Choephoroe;* Euripides, *Iphigenia in Aulis.*

Ajax
: King of Salamis. Recovering his reason after a fit of mental distraction caused by Athena's hatred, he took his own life by the sword. See Sophocles, *Ajax.*

Alcestis
: The "best of women." Wife of Admetus, king of Thessaly, she agreed to die in her husband's place. After her death, Heracles brought her back to life after snatching her from Thanatos (Death). See Euripides, *Alcestis.*

Antigone
: Daughter of Oedipus and Jocasta. When her brothers died in civil strife and mutual suicide, she buried Polynices though forbidden to do so by Creon. Condemned to be walled in, she hanged herself. See Sophocles, *Antigone;* Euripides, *Phoenissae.*

Cassandra
: Daughter of Priam and Hecuba, and a prophetess whom no one believed. She was brought back captive

	to Argos by King Agamemnon and killed with him by Clytemnestra. See Aeschylus, *Agamemnon;* Euripides, *Troades.*
Clytemnestra	Wife of Agamemnon and mother of Iphigenia, Orestes, and Electra. Killed Agamemnon with the help of her lover, Aegisthus. Orestes then killed her with Electra's help. See Aeschylus, *Agamemnon, Choephoroe, Eumenides;* Sophocles, *Electra;* Euripides, *Electra, Iphigenia in Aulis.*
Creon	Brother of Jocasta, husband of Eurydice, father of Haemon and Menoeceus. King of Thebes after the death of the sons of Oedipus. See Sophocles, *Antigone;* Euripides, *Phoenissae.*
Danaids	Daughters of Danaus, who fled from men and marriage. In particular they fled the sons of Aegyptus, their cousins, and were welcomed in Argos by King Pelasgus. See Aeschylus, *Supplices.*
Deianira	Wife of Heracles at Trachis. Sent to the hero the shirt of Nessus, a lover's present she thought, but in fact the cause of his death. Killed herself with a sword. See Sophocles, *Trachiniae.*
Electra	Daughter of Agamemnon and Clytemnestra, she awaited the return of Orestes to avenge their father's death by murdering their mother. See Aeschylus, *Choephoroe;* Sophocles, *Electra;* Euripides, *Electra, Orestes.*
Erechtheus	King of Athens. Sacrificed his daughter or daughters to save the city. See Euripides, *Ion* and the fragments of *Erechtheus.*
Eteocles	Son of Oedipus and Jocasta. Died in the fratricidal combat that opposed him to Polynices. See Aeschylus, *Seven against Thebes;* Euripides, *Phoenissae.*
Eurydice	Wife of Creon and mother of Haemon. On the announcement of her son's suicide, she killed herself with a sword. See Sophocles, *Antigone.*
Evadne	Wife of the hero Capaneus. She threw herself onto the funeral pyre of her husband, who had been killed in front of Thebes. See Euripides, *Suppliant Women.*

Haemon	Son of Creon and Eurydice, and betrothed of Antigone. He killed himself with a sword on discovering Antigone hanged. See Sophocles, *Antigone.*
Hecuba	Wife of Priam, king of Troy, and mother of many children, Cassandra and Polyxena among them. See Euripides, *Troades, Hecuba.*
Helen	The beautiful Helen. Wife of Menelaus, she was carried off by Paris—but some say that only her phantom went to Troy. See Aeschylus, *Agamemnon;* Euripides, *Troades, Helen, Orestes.*
Heracles	The hero of the twelve labors and the husband of many women. In a fit of madness he killed his wife Megara and her children. Killed by the fatal present of Deianira. See Sophocles, *Trachiniae;* Euripides, *Heracles.*
Hermione	Daughter of Menelaus and Helen, wife of Neoptolemus. See Euripides, *Andromache, Orestes.*
Hippolytus	Son of Theseus and the Amazon Antiope. Liked only hunting and the company of Artemis. Phaedra's love and the curse of his father led him to his death. See Euripides, *Hippolytus.*
Hyllus	Son of Heracles and Deianira. See Sophocles, *Trachiniae.*
Iphigenia	Daughter of Agamemnon and Clytemnestra. Sacrificed by her father so that winds should blow and carry the Greek fleet to Troy. In certain tragic versions of the myth she was saved *in extremis* by the goddess Artemis and transported to Tauris, where she presided over human sacrifices until Orestes brought her back to Greece. See Aeschylus, *Agamemnon;* Euripides, *Iphigenia in Aulis, Iphigenia in Tauris.*
Jason	Human, all too human husband of Medea. See Euripides, *Medea.*
Jocasta	Mother and wife of Oedipus, by whom she had two sons, Eteocles and Polynices, and two daughters, one of them Antigone. Killed herself by hanging on discovery of the incest, or by a sword on her sons' death. See Sophocles, *Oedipus Tyrannus;* Euripides, *Phoenissae.*

Leda	Mother of Helen and Clytemnestra. Driven to despair by Helen's bad moral reputation, she hanged herself. See Euripides, *Helen*.
Macaria	Daughter of Heracles. She agreed to be sacrificed to save her brothers. See Euripides, *Heraclidae*.
Medea	Princess of Colchis married to Jason, then abandoned by him for another marriage with the daughter of the king of Corinth. She killed the king and his daughter by poison, and her own children with a sword. See Euripides, *Medea*.
Megara	Faithful wife of Heracles at Thebes. He killed her as well as his children in a fit of madness. See Euripides, *Heracles*.
Menelaus	King of Sparta and husband of Helen. See Euripides, *Troades, Andromache, Helen, Orestes*.
Menoeceus	Son of Creon and brother of Haemon. Committed suicide to save his city. See Euripides, *Phoenissae*.
Neoptolemus	Son of Achilles, on whose tomb he sacrificed Polyxena. Killed at Delphi. See Euripides, *Hecuba, Andromache*.
Oedipus	Son of Laius and Jocasta. Murderer of his father and husband of his mother. Before Jocasta's corpse he blinded himself with the hooks of her dress. His sons killed each other and his daughter Antigone hanged herself. See Sophocles, *Oedipus Tyrannus, Antigone;* Euripides, *Phoenissae*.
Orestes	Son of Agamemnon and Clytemnestra, brother of Iphigenia and Electra. Killed his mother to avenge his father. See Aeschylus, *Choephoroe, Eumenides;* Sophocles, *Electra;* Euripides, *Electra, Iphigenia in Tauris, Orestes*.
Phaedra	The Cretan wife of Theseus. Infatuated with Hippolytus, who only loved the goddess Artemis, she hanged herself. See Euripides, *Hippolytus*.
Polynices	Son of Oedipus and Jocasta. Died in fratricidal combat with his brother, Eteocles. See Aeschylus, *Seven against Thebes;* Euripides, *Phoenissae*.

Polyxena   Daughter of Priam and Hecuba. Sacrificed by Ne-
               optolemus on the tomb of Achilles. See Euripides,
               Troades, Hecuba.

Tecmessa   Companion of Ajax, who reminded her that silence was
               the ornament of women. See Sophocles, *Ajax.*

Teucer   Half-brother of Ajax. See Sophocles, *Ajax.*

Theseus   King of Athens, husband of Phaedra, and father of
               Hippolytus, whom he wrongly cursed. See Euripides,
               Hippolytus.

INDEX